Things which must shortly come to pass

a study of

REVELATION

by

Paul Rose

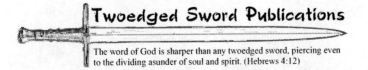

Twoedged Sword Publications

The word of God is sharper than any twoedged sword, piercing even
to the dividing asunder of soul and spirit. (Hebrews 4:12)

Scripture quotations are from the Authorized King James
Version of the Bible (KJV).

ISBN 0-9547205-0-4

Published by Twoedged Sword Publications
PO Box 266, Waterlooville, PO7 5ZT
www.twoedgedswordpublications.co.uk

Dedications

To the glory of God and the extension of His kingdom.

To all those who have endured my preaching from the book of Revelation.

Acknowledgements

My thanks are due to the following people:

Graham Hopkins. It was Graham who first interested me in the book of Revelation and helped me enormously during my early studies. Thank you for many ideas and for many hours of fruitful and interesting discussion.

My wife Jane. Thank you for believing that I could write this book and for initially proof reading it, making suggestions and improvements, and ensuring that I used consistent terminology.

Colin Hopkins. Colin did the second proof reading and checked the references. Thank you for your time, enthusiasm and valued corrections.

Contents

Introduction

Revelation has long interested me. It is a book with so many facets to each description and event that those who study it will see only those which are revealed to them. The same is true of the author; this book shows that which has been revealed to me.

This is a book which has been brewing in my mind throughout the years since my conversion. The material used harks back to my enthusiastic studies during the early years of my Christian life. I hope this work will be of use to Bible students and also that it will help to convince those who do not know the Lord but who nevertheless find the book of Revelation interesting and are not afraid to dig deep and do some soul searching. There are those who come to fear Hell before they come to love Christ. There is a place for conviction through the fear of Hell as well as through the love of Christ. Indeed I came to a saving knowledge of Christ through this route myself. To this end I have seen fit to explain certain things more fully than would be necessary if the book were to be aimed specifically at those who believe already.

The book of Revelation is unique because it is the only apocalyptic writing in the New Testament. An apocalyptic writing is one that is written with pictures and symbols. Other examples are found in Old Testament prophecy. At the time of its writing, people were used to such ways of expression. They knew what the symbolisms stood for, and they knew what should be taken literally. Nowadays however, nobody writes like this, not even in oriental countries, so there is some difficulty in its interpretation.

Christians pay great heed to the New Testament gospels (Matthew, Mark, Luke and John), and to the examples and teaching of the Lord Jesus Christ contained in them, yet the book of Revelation is neglected. It is the same Jesus Christ who has shown us these *...things which must shortly come to pass (Revelation 1:1)*, and yet many Christians have a lack of regard for this book. We really should pay at least the same amount of attention to Revelation as we do to any other book of the Bible; indeed, these things _must_ _shortly_ _come_ _to_ _pass_ and so we should pay the greater heed because of that! We must not be complacent just because this book was written nearly 2000 years ago and the prophesies contained in it do not seem to have happened, (you will see later that many Revelation prophesies have already been fulfilled). This is the kind of revelation that becomes clearer, less obscure and more easily understood as the time for its fulfilment gets ever closer. We know a lot more about its meaning now than we did just 100 years ago. In fact we now know so much of this revelation that those who keep an eye on the political arena can see these things shaping up; they can see the way being prepared for the fulfilment of more Revelation prophecies. In my opinion we should study this book with renewed enthusiasm because these things *must* *shortly* *come* *to* *pass*.

I have tried to keep the book as simple as possible; however, I also want to be reasonably comprehensive, and in the book of Revelation, simplicity and comprehensiveness are often mutually exclusive! Therefore please accept my apologies if you find certain passages difficult to follow. Revelation is a difficult book to understand and I have enjoyed much blessing from the study of it. All who persevere will likewise be blessed (Revelation 1:3). I have found it difficult to maintain a constant tense, especially where Revelation is telling future events but is written in the past or present tense! This is, of course, an indication of the sureness of this prophesy but it does not help the writer maintain good English. Having tried and failed, I have given up on this point, so please also accept my apologies for mixing tenses.

How to read this book

I recommend that each chapter of Revelation is read from the Bible before reading the corresponding chapter in this book. However, I have quoted each Bible passage before commenting on it, so those who do not have a Bible or who prefer to read without reference to their Bible will find it possible to do so. If you follow the second method, please be aware that there are a few verses which I have not quoted or commented on. Particular among these are the various verses describing heavenly worship scenes before God's throne which are really self-explanatory.

So as not to disturb the flow of the narrative, I have used footnotes to draw attention to side issues, quote related Bible passages and for any other additional material. The book can be read without reference to the footnotes, but I have placed them on the same page as the narrative to make it easy for those who wish to refer to them.

1

Revelation chapter 1:
The Revelation of Jesus Christ

[1]How did John receive this revelation?

> *I was in the Spirit on the Lord's day, and heard behind me a great voice, as of a trumpet saying, I am Alpha and Omega, the first and the last: and, What thou seest, write in a book, and send it unto the seven churches which are in Asia; unto Ephesus, and unto Smyrna, and unto Pergamos, and unto Thyatira, and unto Sardis, and unto Philadelphia, and unto Laodicea. And I turned to see the voice that spake with me. And being turned, I saw seven golden candlesticks; And in the midst of the seven candlesticks one like unto the Son of man... (Revelation 1:10-13).*

John was in prayer and received a vision from the Lord Jesus Christ; *and he sent and signified it by his angel unto his servant John (Revelation 1:1)*. The vision was communicated to John by an angel.

Can this revelation be relied upon?

The book starts with the words *The Revelation of Jesus Christ, which God gave unto him, to shew unto his servants things*

---

[1] *Revelation* (Revelation 1:1) literally means 'to reveal' or 'to uncover'. Jesus Christ has revealed this to us via John.

which must shortly come to pass; and he sent and signified it by his angel unto his servant John (Revelation 1:1). The things contained in the book of Revelation have been revealed by Jesus Christ, who sent an angel to communicate these things to John. An angel previously revealed future events to Daniel (Daniel chapters 9 to 12). Daniel did not understand them, nevertheless most of what the angel revealed to him has now been fulfilled, and what remains unfulfilled is what the book of Revelation deals with. The angel that revealed those events to Daniel has been proved reliable. [2]There are also other examples of angels dealings with mankind that can be seen to be reliable as well. So as far as the reliability of the book of Revelation is concerned we can be absolutely certain that these things will happen.

Blessed is he that readeth, and they that hear the words of this prophesy, and keep those things which are written therein (Revelation 1:3)

There is a blessing attached to the reading of this prophetic book:

Firstly, there is a blessing for the reading of this prophesy. The word *readeth* that is used here, literally means 'to know well', which means more than just casual reading. It requires study!

Secondly, this verse continues ...*and they that hear the words of this prophesy.* Again, the word *hear* used, means more than just hearing sounds with the ear: literally translated it means 'to give ear' or 'hearken'. This implies perception and understanding. When a child is reprimanded for doing something wrong and then immediately does the same thing again, the parent might say to

---

[2]Some examples are: Genesis ch 19; Luke 1:5-64; Luke 2:8-16

the child, 'did you hear what I said?' The parent is not asking if
the child heard the sound of the words, but rather, is asking if the
child understood what had been said. So it is here, there is a
blessing not just in hearing the sound of the words, but in the
understanding of it, in the comprehension of this prophesy.

Thirdly, as with the disobedient child, understanding does not
necessarily mean obeying, and this verse goes on to say *...and
keep those things which are written therein*. The blessing comes
from keeping or observing these things. It is necessary that there
is obedience.

So, to sum up, the terms of this blessing are threefold:

1) Study of this prophesy.

2) An understanding, or perception of these things (which
   in turn means that we should be aware of current events
   and watching the way being prepared for the fulfilment
   of this prophesy).

3) Obedience, the keeping of this word. When we
   understand things an obligation is placed upon us.

Of course all three conditions are linked, and if it wasn't for our
fickle human nature, one would naturally lead on to the others.
These are God-given conditions which apply to the book of
Revelation. Interestingly, these same conditions also apply in all
spheres of modern civilization.

Here are two examples:

1) In the medical world there has been a lot of study into
   various life-saving techniques. New drugs, new
   operating techniques, life support machines, and so on.
   Because of this study, doctors have gained an

understanding of new techniques to save peoples lives. So from the study has come understanding, and now because of this understanding, there is a moral obligation to use the knowledge.

Study – Understanding – Obligation.

2) In the last hundred years or so, we have had the benefit of electricity. Its use is now so widespread and people have come to rely so much on a constant supply of electricity that power stations have to be manned twenty-four hours a day, seven days a week to maintain the service. Repair crews also have to be prepared to be called out at any time. Clearly the same conditions apply here too:

Study – Understanding – Obligation.

So these are the conditions for the blessing of verse 3: study, understanding, and the obligation to *keep those things which are written therein.*

The revelation is applicable to the whole church of Christ

John was commanded to write down what he saw in a book and to send it *to the seven churches which are in Asia (Revelation 1:11).* These were of course seven actual churches, but seven is also a number of divine completeness – seven days in a week, therefore every seventh day is the Sabbath (Exodus 20:8-11), every seventh year being the Sabbatical year (Exodus 23:10-11) – so although these were seven actual churches they are representative of the complete church of Christ. These seven churches were commended and reprimanded, as appropriate, by the Lord Jesus Christ. The conditions that existed in these seven churches are representative of the condition of the universal

church throughout the entire [3]church age. The commendations
and reprimands given by Christ to these seven churches are
lessons to be learned by the whole of the church.

God is ever present

John, in his opening greeting, says, *Grace be unto you, and
peace, from him which is, and which was, and which is to come;
and from the seven Spirits which are before his throne
(Revelation 1:4)*. It's interesting how God is described here:
God present, then past, then future. There never has been a time
when God was not there, and there never will be a time when
God will not be there.

Why are there seven Spirits? (Revelation 1:4)

Zechariah 3:9 says: *For behold the stone that I have laid before
Joshua; upon one stone shall be seven eyes: behold, I will
engrave the graving thereof, saith the LORD of hosts, and I will
remove the iniquity of that land in one day*. The stone is Christ,
also referred to as *the headstone* (Zech 4:7). [4]The iniquity of the
land was removed by the sacrifice of Jesus Christ on the cross
of Calvary. The seven eyes are the Holy Spirit and the fact that
upon one stone shall be seven eyes is a reference to the Holy
Spirit lighting upon Christ after He was baptized by John the
Baptist (Matthew 3:16). Christ's later ascension, means that the
Holy Spirit is now present in every believer (John 14:12,16, 26
and John 16:7). In Zechariah 4:10, we are told that *the eyes of*

---

[3]The period in history commencing from the ascension of Christ (Mark 16:19)
until His return to remove His church from the world (1 Cor 15:50-54,
1 Thess 4:13-17, 2 Thess 2:7).

[4]John 3:16-17

the LORD, ...run to and fro through the whole earth.
[5]In 2 Thessalonians 2:7 we are told that the purpose of the Holy
Spirit is to hinder evil. This hindrance of evil is accomplished
by the fact that the Holy Spirit is present in every believer. This
is probably the most important role that the church plays, even
though it is unseen and largely unrealised by the world and even
by the church itself. This is why the [6]tribulation period of seven
years cannot begin until the Holy Spirit is taken out of the earth
when Christ removes His church from the world (this event is
generally known as the Rapture or Translation of the church and
is described in 1 Corinthians 15:51-54 and
1 Thessalonians 4:13-17). Further references to the seven Spirits
are found in Revelation 3:1: *These things saith he that hath the
seven Spirits of God...* and in Revelation 5:6: *the seven eyes,
which are the seven Spirits of God sent forth into all the earth.*

The gospel message (Revelation 1:5)

Jesus Christ, who is the faithful witness (Revelation 1:5)

In the gospels we read that Christ always did the [7]will of His
Father and led a faithful, pure and blameless life. He even did
what is impossible for any ordinary man to do – He lived a
sinless life. He *was in all points tempted like as we are, yet
without sin (Hebrews 4:15).* It was this very sinlessness that
made it possible for Him to *wash... us from our sins in his own*

---

[5]In the KJV of 2 Thess 2:7, the word *letteth* and *let* are used in the Old English
sense of restraining (evil).

[6]This coincides with Daniel's 70th week, Dan 9:27, and is described in detail
later.

[7]e.g. Matthew 26:39

blood (Revelation 1:5). He paid the price for <u>our</u> sins. He who was innocent of all sin, was [8]crucified to pay the [9]price of redemption for our sins. He is *the first begotten of the dead (Revelation 1:5)* or the [10]*firstborn from the dead (Colossians 1:18)*. The Lord Jesus Christ is the only one to have gone through the fulness of this aspect of the divine plan as it is revealed in the Bible: He lived and died on earth; Christ's earthly body was mortal like ours, and because He was raised from the dead then that means that all who belong to Him will be raised from the dead also. This is what it means when it says that He is the *firstborn from the dead* (there will of course be some who will be alive when He returns to take His church out of the world: these will never taste death). So because Christ was raised from the dead as the *firstborn from the dead*, then those who belong to Him will be raised from the dead also, and they will be raised in the same way that He was. It is apparent from the scriptures that when Christ was resurrected He was clothed with a new body, with new powers that mortals do not have. [11]He was able to appear in the middle of a locked room and there are [12]many other differences. When we are resurrected, we too will have the same kind of resurrection body as His (1 Corinthians 15:50-53).

---

[8]Luke 23:33

[9]Titus 2:13-14

[10]See also Luke 24:1-7

[11]John 20:19-31

[12]John 20:30

***And hath made us kings and priests unto God and his Father; to
him be glory and dominion for ever and ever. Amen.
(Revelation 1:6)***

At the moment of Christ's death *the veil of the temple was rent
in twain from the top to the bottom... (Matthew 27:51),*
signifying that access to God is no longer via a [13]priest but is
freely available through the Lord Jesus Christ, every believer
now becoming a priest in his own right. We can now *come
boldly unto the throne of grace (Hebrews 4:16).*

Correct interpretation of the book

The key to the correct interpretation of the book of Revelation is
found in Revelation 1:19 where John is told to *Write the things
which thou hast seen, and the things which are, and the things
which shall be hereafter.* He had to record:

1) That which he had seen, i.e. the vision.

2) The things which are – the letters to the seven churches.

3) The things which shall be hereafter, i.e. after the present
   church age. This starts from Revelation chapter 4.

[14]*Behold, he cometh with clouds... (Revelation 1:7)*

When Christ ascended to the Father (Acts 1:9), the disciples
were told by two angels that when Christ returns at His second

---

[13]A priest is essentially a mediator between man and God. See Leviticus 16:3-19
for a description of the high priest's entry into the holy place within the veil.

[14] See also Zechariah chapter 12

coming, also known as the second advent, it will be in the same
way that the disciples saw Him received into Heaven
(Acts 1:10-11), i.e. with clouds. Revelation 1:7 reaffirms this
statement. He will not return in lowly manner like His first
advent when He was born as a baby in Bethlehem
(Matthew 2:1) but [15]He will return as a conquering King and we
are told that *every eye shall see him....* [16]It is impossible to say
whether man's technology (e.g. satellite television) will play a
part here, or whether it will be by wholly divine means. At His
second advent all mankind, both dead and alive, will know Him
for who He is. Those who crucified Him, now long dead, will
see Him, as will those still alive at His coming.

The mystery of the seven stars... and the seven golden candlesticks (Revelation 1:12-13, 20)

At the voice of Christ in his vision, John turned and *saw seven
golden candlesticks; and in the midst of the seven candlesticks
one like unto the Son of man... and he had in his right hand
seven stars (Revelation 1:12,13,16).* We are told in verse 20
what these objects symbolise: *The seven stars are the angels of
the seven churches: and the seven candlesticks... are the seven*

---

[15]Matthew 24:29-31

[16]God frequently uses man's technology to bring about events. For example,
healing now comes via medicine, with God imparting wisdom to doctors and
nurses in answer to prayer, as well as by direct miraculous means. In olden times
when medical practice was not as advanced as it is today, healing by obvious
miraculous means was much more prevalent. However as medical practice has
improved it is evident that God's healing power is used through medicine,
miraculous healing being seen less often. This is not to say that God is not at
work in this realm, just that where man has the means to accomplish events, God
often works through the devices of man. This happens in all spheres of activity,
not just in healing. As a general rule: God does not seem to do what man can do
for himself.

churches. Stars and *Candlesticks* provide light in the spiritual darkness of the world. They are symbols of God's people, [17]who reflect Christ's light. The angels (the literal translation is 'messenger' or 'agent') may not have been angelic beings but agents sent to John by these churches.

John's vision of Christ

And I turned to see the voice that spake with me. And being turned, I saw seven golden candlesticks; And in the midst of the seven candlesticks one like unto the Son of man, clothed with a garment down to the foot, and girt about the paps with a golden girdle. His head and his hairs were white like wool, as white as snow; and his eyes were as a flame of fire; And his feet like unto fine brass, as if they burned in a furnace; and his voice as the sound of many waters. And he had in his right hand seven stars: and out of his mouth went a sharp twoedged sword: and his countenance was as the sun shineth in his strength. (Revelation 1:12-16)

John sees [18]Christ in the midst of His church, symbolised by the seven golden candlesticks. The garment He wears and the golden girdle show His [19]priesthood, He is our [20]great high priest. [21]His snow white hair portrays His eternal existence. His flaming eyes symbolise Christ as Judge. His feet *like unto fine*

---

[17]John 8:12, 9:5

[18]Compare Matthew 18:20

[19]Exodus 28:4

[20]Hebrews 4:14

[21]Daniel 7:9, See also John 1:1-14

brass, as if they burned in a furnace are the same feet that
[22]*treadeth the wine-press of the fierceness and wrath of
Almighty God* at the battle of Armageddon. His voice, was *as
the sound of many waters... and out of his mouth went a sharp
twoedged sword (Revelation 1:15-16)* showing that He is the
source of life to His followers, water being a source of life, and
also speaks of His victory at the battle of Armageddon where
His weapon is this same sword, i.e. His word. He has but to
speak and His enemies are conquered. The word that He speaks
is the [23]word of God. His *countenance... as the sun* shows Jesus
in His glory. In Matthew 16:28, Jesus said to His disciples
*...there be some standing here, which shall not taste of death,
till they see the Son of man coming in His kingdom.* This
prediction was fulfilled six days later when Peter, James and
John witnessed His transfiguration with Moses and Elijah
(Mt 17:1-3). [24]This transfiguration before the three disciples was
a portrayal of that which was to come, recorded here in
Revelation 1:16.

*And when I saw him, I fell at his feet as dead. And he laid his
right hand upon me, saying unto me, Fear not; I am the first and
the last: I am he that liveth, and was dead; and, behold, I am alive
for evermore, Amen; and have the keys of hell and of death.
(Revelation 1:17-18)*

John is terrified at the sight of His resurrected and glorified
Saviour and prostrates himself until comforted by Christ, who
has the *keys of hell and of death (Revelation 1:18).* The keys are

---

[22]Revelation 19:15, 21

[23]Ephesians 6:17, Hebrews 4:12

[24]2 Peter 1:16-18

emblems of authority and access. Having conquered death, He alone can open and shut the gates of Hell.

2

Revelation chapter 2:
The letters to the seven churches –
Ephesus, Smyrna, Pergamos, Thyatira

Some general points

The letters were written to seven actual churches; however, the lessons revealed are applicable to the whole church of Christ. Every letter starts with a commendation before going on to reveal what is wrong. Only two of the letters find no fault with the churches concerned: Smyrna – the church under persecution, and Philadelphia – the church in revival.

Ephesus (Revelation 2:1-7)

Ephesus was a port city of Ionia (a Greek district of Asia Minor), located near modern Izmir, Turkey, at the mouth of the Cayster (Küçükmenderes) River and was a major departure point for trade routes into Asia Minor. It was known for its shrines to the goddess Artemis, or Diana. Ephesus came under Roman rule in 189 BC and remained an important commercial centre.

Unto the angel of the church of Ephesus write; These things saith he that holdeth the seven stars in his right hand, who walketh in the midst of the seven golden candlesticks; I know thy works, and thy labour, and thy patience, and how thou canst not bear them which are evil: and thou hast tried them which say they are

*apostles, and are not, and hast found them liars: And hast borne,
and hast patience, and for my name's sake hast laboured, and
hast not fainted (Revelation 2:1-3)*

There couldn't possibly be anything wrong with a church like that,
could there? Let us read more of Christ's account of this church:

***Nevertheless I have somewhat against thee, because thou hast left
thy first love. Remember therefore from whence thou art fallen,
and repent, and do the first works; or else I will come unto thee
quickly, and will remove thy candlestick out of his place, except
thou repent (Revelation 2:4-5)***

Despite all their good works and achievements, the Ephesians
were in danger of having their church removed by God. Why,
what was their sin?: *...because thou hast left thy first love
(Revelation 2:4)*. It perhaps doesn't seem a bad sin; they did all
the right things. To the onlooker it probably seemed a thriving
church, but they had left their first love. If you are a Christian,
do you remember the time when you first gave yourself to the
Lord? What JOY, what NEW LIFE welled up within you. Do
you remember when you hung on every word of the Bible,
when every day you learnt more and more about God and about
the Lord Jesus Christ? What enthusiasm you had for the things
of God! It was like that for the Ephesians at first, but then their
keen enthusiasm had waned. The fire that burned in their hearts

---

[1] There is no case for apostleship outside of the twelve apostles of the Bible. The
church at Ephesus was troubled by those who claimed to be apostles, and *found
them liars*; modern day churches also, especially those of the charismatic
persuasion, have among them those who profess to be modern day apostles. It is
worth noting Revelation 21:14 *And the wall of the city had twelve foundations,
and in them the names of **the twelve apostles of the Lamb*** (my emphasis). There
are no apostles other than the twelve apostles of the Bible.

so fiercely had died to a mere smoulder. Perhaps worldly cares and pleasures became more important to them.

What had they to do to put things right? *Remember therefore from whence thou art fallen, and repent, and do the first works (Revelation 2:5).*

What would happen if they continued in their loveless way? *...I will come unto thee quickly, and will remove thy candlestick out of his place, except thou repent (Revelation 2:5).* The church at Ephesus would be removed unless they rekindled their love for the Lord!

But this thou hast, that thou hatest the deeds of the Nicolaitans, which I also hate. (Revelation 2:6)

The Nicolaitans were the followers of Nicolas; his exact doctrine we are not told, except that in Revelation 2:14-15 the Lord equates it with the doctrine of Balaam. See later text on the church at Pergamos for a description of the doctrine of Balaam.

Smyrna (Revelation 2:8-11)

Smyrna is now the city of Izmir, Turkey. It is still an important commercial centre. Smyrna had many religious cults, including that of Caesar worship. The Jews of the city made life very difficult for the Christians there.

And unto the angel of the church in Smyrna write; These things saith the first and the last, which was dead, and is alive; I know thy works, and tribulation, and poverty, (but thou art rich) and I know the blasphemy of them which say they are Jews, and are not, but are the synagogue of Satan. Fear none of those things

which thou shalt suffer: behold, the devil shall cast some of you into prison, that ye may be tried; and ye shall have tribulation ten days: be thou faithful unto death, and I will give thee a crown of life. (Revelation 2:8-10)

There is no word of condemnation to this persecuted church. The Jews of the city blasphemed Christ and so were given the name of *the synagogue of Satan (Revelation 2:9)*. The Lord said to the church *Fear none of those things which thou shalt suffer: behold the devil shall cast some of you into prison, that ye may be tried* [tempted to renounce their faith]*; and ye shall have tribulation ten days: be thou faithful unto death, and I will give thee a crown of life (Revelation 2:10)*. In Hebrews chapter 11 there is a list of people, some of whom God made to triumph over their trials, while *others were tortured, not accepting deliverance. And others had trial of cruel mockings and scourgings, yea, moreover of bonds and imprisonment: They were stoned, they were sawn asunder, were tempted, were slain with the sword... (Heb 11:35-37)*. In Acts chapter 12 we are told that James was killed by Herod, but God delivered Peter from Herod. It is a mystery why some churches suffer persecution and others do not, yet God is a part of both. God did not rescue James, but He did rescue Peter. Some churches suffer terribly for their faith, others don't. Some Christians will be troubled, persecuted, harassed and abused because of their faith, other Christians will escape such things. That is not to say that either party is better or more faithful than the other. God alone knows why this is so. Whether we suffer for Christ's sake, like the church at Smyrna, or whether we have it comparatively easy, there is a reward to those who *overcome* or 'gain the victory'. Revelation 3:12 says, *Him that overcometh will I make a pillar in the temple of my God, and he shall go no more out: and I will write upon him the name of my God, and the name of the city of my God, which is new Jerusalem, which cometh down out of heaven from my God: and I will write upon him my new name.*

He that overcometh shall not be hurt of the second death (Revelation 2:11)

We are told what the second death is in Revelation 20:10-15. This subject will be covered in more detail later in the book, but briefly, the second death is the lake of fire, the place of everlasting torment.

And death and hell were cast into the lake of fire. This is the second death. And whosoever was not found written in the book of life was cast into the lake of fire (Revelation 20:14-15).

...the fearful, and unbelieving, and the abominable, and murderers, and whoremongers, and sorcerers, and idolaters, and all liars, shall have their part in the lake which burneth with fire and brimstone: which is the second death (Revelation 21:8).

Pergamos (Revelation 2:12-17)

Pergamos was located on the Aegean sea about 60 miles north of Smyrna. It was an idolatrous city with temples dedicated to Greek gods. Caesar worship was also practised.

And to the angel of the church in Pergamos write; These things saith he which hath the sharp sword with two edges; I know thy works, and where thou dwellest, even where Satan's seat is: and thou holdest fast my name, and hast not denied my faith, even in those days wherein Antipas was my faithful martyr, who was slain among you, where Satan dwelleth. But I have a few things against thee, because thou hast there them that hold the doctrine of Balaam, who taught Balac to cast a stumblingblock before the children of Israel, to eat things sacrificed unto idols, and to commit fornication. So hast thou also them that hold the doctrine of the Nicolaitans, which thing I hate. Repent; or else I will come unto thee quickly, and will fight against them with the sword of my mouth. He that hath an ear, let him hear what the Spirit saith unto the churches; To him that overcometh will I give to eat of the hidden manna, and will give him a white stone, and in the stone a new name written, which no man knoweth saving he that receiveth it. (Revelation 2:12-17)

I know...where Satan's seat is (Revelation 2:13)

The apostle Paul says, in 1 Corinthians 10:19-20 *What say I then? that the idol is anything, or that which is offered in sacrifice to idols is anything? But I say, that the things which the Gentiles sacrifice, they sacrifice to devils, and not to God...* So what is referred to as *Satan's seat* (the literal translation is 'Satan's throne') was the idol worship that abounded in that place. It was a real stronghold of Satan!

The Nicolaitans

The Nicolaitans were the followers of Nicolas; his exact doctrine we are not told, except that in Revelation 2:14-15 the Lord equates it with the doctrine of Balaam.

...thou hast there them that hold the doctrine of Balaam, who taught Balac to cast a stumblingblock before the children of Israel... (Revelation 2:14)

[2]It would appear that Balaam started his prophetic ministry as a godly man. At first impression we have little evidence to think badly of him. Balak was the king of Moab and he wanted Balaam to curse Israel because Israel had come to the borders of his land

---

[2]Numbers chapters 22, 23, 24, Num.25:1-9, Num.31:16; 2 Pet.2:15-16.

and he saw that the Israelites would be too great for him in a battle. Balak had sent his princes to bring Balaam to curse Israel. God told Balaam not to go and Balaam refused to go with them. So Balak sent more princes to him, and once again, by the mouth of the Lord, Balaam had refused to go with them; but they had stayed overnight and the Lord had said to Balaam that he could go with them if they came for him again, but in the morning, without waiting for them to come to him, Balaam saddled his ass and went with them. On the way to Balak, the angel of the Lord intercepted him. He was allowed to continue by the Lord's permissive, rather than directive, will, and was commanded to speak only the word of the Lord. Three times Balak had brought Balaam to a different vantage point where he could see the camp of the Israelites, offered burnt sacrifices and wanted Balaam to curse Israel. But Balaam spoke only what the Lord put into his mouth, which was that Israel was blessed and all those who cursed Israel were cursed. As the story unfolds however, we learn more about Balaam. Although he portrayed his ministry as a prophet of God, he desired reward for his services [3](unlike true prophets of God). He was anxious to please men for *rewards of divination* (cp. Num 22:7, Jude 11); when Balak sent him away empty-handed saying *the Lord hath kept thee back from honour (Num 24:11)*, Balaam was very anxious to please Balak to obtain some reward for his hire, so that at the last, he told Balak how to bring the Israelites low for a time by tempting them into marriage with Midianite women. The Israelites were enticed away from their walk with God, into licentious idolatry. This caused God to destroy 24,000 Israelites to rid them of that idolatrous curse (Num 25:1-9, 31:16).

---

[3] Abram – Genesis 14:22-23, Elisha – 2 Kings 5:15-16, Daniel – though he received great gifts and honours from Nebuchadnezzar, never desired them but rather had them thrust upon him, and was able to use them in God's service.

Certainly there is a warning of worldliness in the church here, of which we are told in James 4:4 *...know ye not that the friendship of the world is enmity with God? Whosoever therefore will be a friend of the world is the enemy of God*; e.g. the example of Balaam who enticed the people away from God and into conformity with the world.

However this is not the main thrust of this letter. The church at Pergamos had amongst them, those who held to, and taught, the same kind of doctrine as Balaam taught:

1) *to eat things sacrificed unto idols (Revelation 2:14)*

2) *to commit fornication (Revelation 2:14)*

3) *to commit whoredom with the daughters of Moab (Num 25:1)*

Let us look at each of these in turn:

1) *to eat things sacrificed unto idols (Revelation 2:14)*

The apostle Paul says, in 1 Corinthians 10:19-20 *What say I then? that the idol is anything, or that which is offered in sacrifice to idols is anything? But I say, that the things which the Gentiles sacrifice, they sacrifice to devils, and not to God...*

The sin of eating things sacrificed unto idols, is in the identifying with the idol. As an example let us consider the [4]feast of the Passover. In eating the Passover lamb the people remember how the Lord brought them out of [5]Egypt. They

---

[4]Exodus 12:25-28

[5]Exodus, chapters 3 to 14.

identify themselves with the Lord God. They say in their heart, Yes the Lord is good, I believe what He says, He is my God, I identify myself with Him and His doctrine. Those at Pergamos who were eating things sacrificed to idols were identifying themselves with the idols in the same way. It wasn't just a case of buying a piece of meat at the market which had been sacrificed to an idol. The context is like the Passover festival, except that these were festivals or feasts dedicated to idols. The people attending these idol feasts would be identifying themselves with the idol, and with that particular doctrine. This is what the Pergamos Balaamites were teaching and encouraging the church at Pergamos to do. This is comparable to modern day teachers of the liberal gospel. Teachers drawing people away from God by explaining away 'inconvenient' portions of God's word. Teaching their own doctrine and 'interpreting' the Bible to suit their own doctrine and their own lifestyle. Just as the Israelites were drawn away from God into the sexual rites of the worship of the idol Baal-Peor, so too, [6]these false teachers have lifestyles that are lustful and sensual; and their doctrine has to justify their lifestyle. This is what the false teachers in the church at Pergamos were like, and false teachers are just the same today, creeping into our churches: into positions of authority, into congregations, enticing people to their own doctrine. The same kind of men who taught the church at Pergamos to identify with idols, are present in our churches today, enticing men and women away from the true worship of God.

---

[6]See Jude 4, 7, 8, 11, 12, 13, 16-19

2) *to commit fornication (Revelation 2:14)*

The meaning here is twofold – both physical and spiritual:

Physical, because these teachers have a sensual lifestyle. Their doctrine agrees with this and they encourage others to conform to their standard.

Spiritual, because whenever a Christian has an idol, there is spiritual fornication. We are considering <u>fornication</u>, not adultery. From a spiritual aspect the church is betrothed to Christ but the marriage does not take place until after the [7]rapture, or translation of the church. Some Bible translations do not differentiate between fornication and adultery. However there is a difference: adultery takes place when one or both persons are married; fornication takes place where both persons are unmarried. The word 'adultery' is often used in the Old Testament because of the Jewish marriage custom where they had a period of [8]betrothal. The betrothed couple were considered virtually married. She was considered to be his wife; he was considered to be her husband, even though no marriage ceremony had taken place, and even though they lived in separate houses. It was almost unheard of for a betrothal to be broken off. That is why in the Old Testament a broken off betrothal was considered a 'divorce', and why the word 'adultery' is often used where, strictly speaking, according to our western ways, the word 'fornication' would actually be correct. This confusion happens less in the New Testament, but care is still needed where the word 'adultery' is used.

---

[7] 1 Cor 15:50-54, 1 Thess 4:13-17, 2 Thess 2:7

[8] Unlike an engagement which may be broken off, a betrothal was considered absolutely binding.

We have already seen how these Balaamites, or false teachers, lead people away from true doctrine and entice them into conformity with their own doctrine and their own standards. Conformation to any standard other than God's is idolatry. For a Christian to do this is also spiritual fornication.

3) ...*the people began to commit whoredom with the daughters of Moab (Numbers 25:1)*

Balaam taught Balak how to turn the Israelites away from God by enticing them into marriages with the women of Moab and Midian.

In Deuteronomy 7:3-4, God says concerning the other nations: *neither shalt thou make marriages with them; thy daughter thou shalt not give unto his son, nor his daughter shalt thou take unto thy son. For they will turn away thy son from following me, that they may serve other gods...*

King Solomon had 700 wives, even though Deuteronomy 17:17 forbids a king to have more than one wife. Many of them were from other nations; 1 Kings 11:4 says ...*it came to pass, when Solomon was old, that his wives turned away his heart after other gods...*

God recognises that the marriage of the godly with the ungodly cannot work. We are warned about it in the New Testament too:

Be ye not unequally yoked together with unbelievers: for what fellowship hath righteousness with unrighteousness? and what communion hath light with darkness? And what concord hath Christ with Belial? or what part hath he that believeth with an infidel? And what agreement hath the temple of God with idols? for ye are the temple of the living God; as God hath said, I will dwell in them; and I will be their God, and they shall be my people. Wherefore come out from among them, and be ye separate, saith the Lord, and touch not the unclean thing; and I will receive you, and will be a Father unto you, and ye shall be my sons and daughters, saith the Lord Almighty. (2 Cor 6:14-18).

The marriage of God's people with non-believers has been a problem throughout history: in the Old Testament, in the early church, and still now. It is something which the world sees nothing wrong with, but for the Christian, it is at best the start of a compromised walk. Whatever the end result, for the Christian it is idolatry. By disobeying God on this point, he or she is holding that other person in higher regard than God. For the Christian it is also fornication in God's eyes: the text for this section was from Numbers 25:1 ...*the people began to commit whoredom with the daughters of Moab.* The word *whoredom* used here is the same word that is translated 'fornication' elsewhere. Its literal meaning is 'to commit fornication'.

To him that overcometh will I give to eat of the hidden manna, and will give him a white stone, and in the stone a new name written, which no man knoweth saving he that receiveth it (Revelation 2:17)

Overcomers will be given spiritual food, described as *hidden manna.* A white stone among the Romans was a sign of joyfulness. To receive a white stone from our heavenly Father is indeed a joyous welcome to a new home in Heaven.

Thyatira (Revelation 2:18-29)

Thyatira was located on an important trade route on the Lycus river, 27 miles from Sardis. [9]Dyeing was an important industry in this commercial centre which was riddled with pagan religion. Thyatira had a busy church. Christ commends their works, charity, service, faith and patience. Indeed it seems from Revelation 2:19 that their works were increasing.

*And unto the angel of the church in Thyatira write; These things saith the Son of God, who hath his eyes like unto a flame of fire, and his feet are like fine brass; I know thy works, and charity, and service, and faith, and thy patience, and thy works; and the last to be more than the first. Notwithstanding I have a few things against thee, because thou sufferest that woman Jezebel, which calleth herself a prophetess, to teach and to seduce my servants to commit fornication, and to eat things sacrificed unto idols. And I gave her space to repent of her fornication; and she repented not. Behold, I will cast her into a bed, and them that commit adultery with her into great tribulation, except they repent of their deeds. And I will kill her children with death; and all the churches shall know that I am he which searcheth the reins and hearts: and I will give unto every one of you according to your works. But unto you I say, and unto the rest in Thyatira, as many as have not this doctrine, and which have not known the depths of Satan, as they speak; I will put upon you none other burden. But that which ye have already hold fast till I come. And he that overcometh, and keepeth my works unto the end, to him will I give power over the nations: And he shall rule them with a rod of iron; as the vessels of a potter shall they be broken to shivers: even as I received of my Father. And I will give him the morning star.
(Revelation 2:18-28)*

---

[9]Acts 16:14

33

*...thou sufferest that woman Jezebel, which calleth herself a
prophetess, to teach and to seduce my servants to commit
fornication, and to eat things sacrificed unto idols
(Revelation 2:20)*

The Jezebel in Revelation is so named because she resembles
[10]Jezebel the Phoenician princess who married king Ahab. Ahab
was like [11]putty in the hands of his wife, Jezebel. [12]When Ahab
planted a grove and built an altar to Baal, it was Jezebel who
had incited him to do it. Because of her position as queen, and
because of her strong character and single-mindedness she was
very influential. If Jezebel wanted something, she got it, with or
without Ahab's knowledge! [13]It was Jezebel who had Naboth
murdered, even though she had written the instructions in
Ahab's name, and sealed them with Ahab's seal. When the word
came that Naboth was dead, the messengers returned, not to
king Ahab, but to [14]Jezebel. There was much to be admired in
Jezebel: strong character, single-minded, determined,
influential, but alas it was directed toward evil and not good.
Notice too that when she revealed to Ahab that Naboth was
dead, and told him to go and take possession of Naboth's
vineyard, we read nothing of Ahab questioning his wife; he just
went at her bidding and took possession.

---

[10]1 Kings 16:31

[11]1 Kings 21:25

[12]1 Kings 16:31-33

[13]1 Kings chapter 21

[14]1 Kings 21:14

We can see how determined and single-minded she was from the affair on [15]Mt. Carmel. It was Jezebel who had influenced Ahab to worship Baal. [16]Jezebel herself was the head of the 450 prophets of Baal and the 400 prophets of the groves. The prophet Elijah demonstrated the power of God by setting up a sacrifice, drenching it with water, and then praying that God Himself would provide the fire to burn the sacrifice. The fire of the Lord fell and consumed the sacrifice proving that the Lord was the true God and that Baal was a fake. The people turned from Baal and worshipped God. When the news was broken to Jezebel however, and when she learned that her prophets had all been killed, she was not panicked into turning from worshipping Baal. Instead she threatened Elijah with his life, and her reputation was such that even though Elijah seemed to have the advantage, he fled for his life!

The Jezebel in Revelation had these same qualities and traits and it seems that she was worse in God's eyes than Balaam (cp. Revelation 2:14, Revelation 2:20-23). Balaam fell because of his desire for money and popularity. Jezebel's motives were different, she had no lack of money, she had power and influence. Her determination was that idols would be worshipped and that the people would follow evil, and corrupt themselves by worshipping false gods. Balaam really meant no evil to the Israelites, but was overcome by the temptation of obtaining some reward for his hire when he counselled Balak about how to bring the Israelites low by enticing them with Midianite women. Jezebel however, purposely set out to deprave the Israelites with the vile rites of the Phoenician gods and hence her sin was accounted worse than that of Balaam's.

---

[15]1 Kings 18:17-40

[16]1 Kings 18:19

We can see how great her power and influence was in the church at Thyatira by Revelation 2:24-25, *But unto you I say, and unto the rest in Thyatira, as many as have not this doctrine, and which have not known the depths of Satan, as they speak; I will put upon you none other burden. But that which ye have already hold fast till I come.* God could not expect spiritual growth in a church with this kind of influence in it. They would do well even to maintain their present standards and not decline.

Jezebel used the weakness of her husband to obtain what she wanted, and to establish the religion that she wanted to impose upon the people. Likewise the Jezebels in our churches use the weaknesses of the church to influence the doctrine, direction, and vision of the church.

In Revelation 2:21, Jezebel was called upon to repent. She didn't, just as Jezebel, wife of Ahab, did not repent when she had opportunity to turn from Baal and follow the Lord. The same will be true for the Jezebels in our churches today. They are deliberately corrupting Christians and undermining the work of the church; leading them into doctrines and practices which not only displease God but which are described as *fornication* and *adultery*. These Jezebels know what they are and what they are doing; that is why they are so dangerous in our churches. They will not repent and neither is it possible to be rid of them, that is apparent from the [17]parable of the wheat and tares, the tares are to be left to grow with the wheat and it is not until the harvest that they can be safely parted. That the Jezebels in our churches are dangerous is evident from the punishment that will be their's and their follower's, described in Revelation 2:22-23. It will not be until the [18]rapture of the church that we will know

---

[17]Matthew 13:24-30, 13:36-43

[18]1 Cor 15:50-54, 1 Thess 4:13-17, 2 Thess 2:7

the extent of their infiltration in our churches, because when the church is taken up to be with the Lord, they will be left to go *into great tribulation (Revelation 2:22).*

The Jezebel of the tribulation period

When the true church is removed from the world (i.e. at the rapture), there will remain on earth all the false elements of the church. This false church is described In Revelation chapters 13, 17 and 18. It is too complex to enter into any details now, but you may like to compare the second beast of Revelation chapter 13, generally known as the False Prophet (Revelation 13:11-18), with Jezebel. They are remarkably similar, especially in regard to deception and the ability to incite others to idolatry.

3

Revelation chapter 3:
The letters to the seven churches –
Sardis, Philadelphia, Laodicea

Sardis (Revelation 3:1-6)

Located 50 miles north-east of Smyrna, Sardis was noted for its wealth because of its textile and jewellery industries. The art of dyeing wool may have been invented there.

And unto the angel of the church in Sardis write; These things saith he that hath the seven Spirits of God, and the seven stars; I know thy works, that thou hast a name that thou livest, and art dead. Be watchful, and strengthen the things which remain, that are ready to die: for I have not found thy works perfect before God. Remember therefore how thou hast received and heard, and hold fast, and repent. If therefore thou shalt not watch, I will come on thee as a thief, and thou shalt not know what hour I will come upon thee. Thou hast a few names even in Sardis which have not defiled their garments; and they shall walk with me in white: for they are worthy. He that overcometh, the same shall be clothed in white raiment; and I will not blot out his name out of the book of life, but I will confess his name before my Father, and before his angels. He that hath an ear, let him hear what the Spirit saith unto the churches. (Revelation 3:1-6)

These things saith he that hath the seven Spirits of God, and the seven stars... (Revelation 3:1)

For an explanation of the term *the seven Spirits of God*, see chapter one: 'Why are there seven Spirits? (Revelation 1:4)'.

The *seven stars* are also covered in chapter one: 'The mystery of the seven stars... and the seven golden candlesticks (Revelation 1:12-13, 20)'.

In His opening greeting, the Lord was painting a picture to those believers in Sardis, portraying to them the fact that He is there with them, not just as an observer, but actually in the midst of them, knowing the thoughts and intents of each one; knowing also how the world around saw them. He was giving them the realization of His intimate knowledge of them, and of the falsehood of their reputation in the world. He finished His greeting by declaring His knowledge of their situation: *I know thy works, that thou hast a name that thou livest, and art dead (Revelation 3:1)*.

If therefore thou shalt not watch, I will come on thee as a thief, and thou shalt not know what hour I will come upon thee (Revelation 3:3)

[1]This is a reference to the rapture, or translation of the church, when the Holy Spirit, along with the church, is taken out of the world prior to the start of the tribulation period. The Holy Spirit's removal from the world is the warning that the Lord gave to those Christians in Sardis who were not watching and waiting for that momentous occasion that every Christian should be ready for!

---

[1] 1 Cor.15:50-54, 1 Thess.4:13-17, 2 Thess.2:7

Thou hast a few names even in Sardis which have not defiled their garments; and they shall walk with me in white: for they are worthy. He that overcometh, the same shall be clothed in white raiment (Revelation 3:4-5)

The description of the church at Sardis is very much like some modern churches, where although there are a few genuine believers, there are many more nominal members. Nowadays we tend to regard 'nominal Christians' as Christian in name but not genuine believers: those who have attached the name of Christianity to themselves, for whatever reason, but who are unregenerate. However the majority of the nominal members at Sardis were of a different kind. They were genuine believers but they were compromising with the world. In their day and situation it would be madness to label themselves 'Christian' if they were not genuine disciples! Their situation was quite desperate: they had to live up to Christ's standards in a city that was wholly idolatrous and promiscuous.

The early church was under terrific pressure to conform. Living in towns where many different gods, including Caesar, were worshipped, Christians would even find it hard to buy [2]meat that hadn't been sacrificed to a pagan god. Worship of many of the idols involved sexual promiscuity. This was normal rather than exceptional! Those who didn't conform to the values of this idolatrous age were regarded as peculiar and would be shunned, even to the point where their livelihood would be severely affected.

Many of those in the church at Sardis had compromised their walk. As well as what they might call their 'show' of idolatry, they were persuaded into promiscuous idolatry in order to

---

[2]See 1 Corinthians 10:25-28

safeguard their livelihood. This is what life was like in Sardis for a Christian. That church, although not under actual persecution, was under terrific pressure to conform. The pressure to conform in our own time is quite different, and yet is it? The actual details may differ, the rules of conformity may differ, but they are still there although the pressure is more subtle. The pagans at Sardis, for all their religious pretensions, were trying to fill that void that only Christ can fill, in the same way that people do today – by diversions and entertainment. The diversions and entertainment may be different now, but they are still there. This area is a difficult one for the Christian to come to terms with; we can't cut ourselves off from it entirely, and neither should we try to; that would mean the life of a recluse – a trap which some Christian denominations have fallen into nevertheless. But if we have no contact with the world then we have no testimony to the unbeliever. And besides, that is not the way that the Lord demonstrated to us while He was in the world. He didn't cut Himself off from the unbeliever, and neither should we. Neither should we join in with the world's activities with the abandon that we see many unbelievers exhibiting. However, it would be wrong for us to lay down the [3]law as to what a Christian should and should not allow. I do not mean adultery, or drunkenness, or anything else that the Bible clearly states is wrong; but it would be wrong for us to put a blanket ban on, say, television or sport. Each Christian should prayerfully consider what he should allow and what he ought to shun. The list will not be the same for everyone; what one Christian may allow, another may be called to shun. There are many grey areas: Should a Christian watch television or go to the cinema? Should he drink alcohol or

---

[3] To add to the prohibitions of God's law was one of the chief mistakes of the Pharisees, e.g. Matthew 12:1-5, 15:1-9.

smoke? Should he go to the theatre? Should he play football?
The list is a long one.

The dangers are quite subtle: in so many areas of entertainment
the message is the same as in Sardis. The world preaches
'freedom', but this so called freedom that we are called to
indulge in, is really conformity – conformity to the world's
standards. The call is to enjoy ourselves now, and not to think
of the consequences. They, apparently, will take care of
themselves. The dangers are not always obvious. We may shun
sex and violence on the television screen, but we can still be
open to subtle dangers: the veneer of glamour portrayed in some
programmes, or the so-called freedom and happiness of the
promiscuous lifestyle portrayed by some others; or even the
seemingly innocent 'happy ever after' scenario.

There is also the danger that when we try not to cut ourselves
off from the world we may go too far and get so wrapped up in
the things of the world that God gets squeezed out. With so
much time spent in various activities, there is the danger that we
may, unconsciously at first, spend less time in prayer, or in
reading and studying God's word, until it becomes sporadic, and
then maybe stops altogether, except on Sunday at the church
service. When worldly things start to squeeze God out of a
Christian's life he has started on the slippery slope of idolatry.
The things that mean so much to the Christian, that he is
prepared to compromise his Christian devotions, become idols
and the Christian's walk is compromised. It is not far removed
from bowing to a pagan god in Sardis.

To the Lord Jesus Christ a compromised walk is not good
enough. The church at Sardis were told to *be watchful* [or
vigilant], *and strengthen the things which remain, that are
ready to die (Revelation 3:2).*

*He that saith, I Know him, and keepeth not his commandments,
is a liar, and the truth is not in him. But whoso keepeth his
word, in him verily is the love of God perfected: hereby know
we that we are in him. He that saith he abideth in him ought
himself also so to walk, even as he walked (1 John 2:4-6).*

Philadelphia (Revelation 3:7-13)

Located 25 miles south-east of Sardis and 952 feet above sea
level, the city became an important commercial centre despite
constant and severe earthquakes which threatened its
destruction. The city was constantly being repaired at great
cost due to the earthquakes. The site of the ancient city is
occupied by the modern city Alasehir, Turkey.

*And to the angel of the church in Philadelphia write; These
things saith he that is holy, he that is true, he that hath the key of
David, he that openeth, and no man shutteth; and shutteth, and
no man openeth; I know thy works: behold, I have set before thee
an open door, and no man can shut it: for thou hast a little
strength, and hast kept my word, and hast not denied my name.
Behold, I will make them of the synagogue of Satan, which say
they are Jews, and are not, but do lie; behold, I will make them to
come and worship before thy feet, and to know that I have loved
thee. Because thou hast kept the word of my patience, I also will
keep thee from the hour of temptation, which shall come upon all
the world, to try them that dwell upon the earth. Behold, I come
quickly: hold that fast which thou hast, that no man take thy
crown. Him that overcometh will I make a pillar in the temple of
my God, and he shall go no more out: and I will write upon him
the name of my God, and the name of the city of my God, which is
new Jerusalem, which cometh down out of heaven from my God:
and I will write upon him my new name. He that hath an ear, let
him hear what the Spirit saith unto the churches.
(Revelation 3:7-13)*

These things saith he that is holy, he that is true, he that hath the key of David, he that openeth and no man shutteth; and shutteth and no man openeth (Revelation 3:7)

The letter is addressed to this church proclaiming these particular virtues of Christ: that he is *holy* which means 'separate' or 'set apart'; that he is *true*, signifying that He is the truth; that He *hath the key of David*, signifying His kingly authority; and that He *openeth and no man shutteth; and shutteth and no man openeth* showing that He has absolute control over the affairs of men.

I have set before thee an open door (Revelation 3:8)

This is a growing church, a church in revival! The Lord knows their works and is pleased. He has set before them *...an open door, and no man can shut it (Revelation 3:8)*. Christ has prepared the way before His faithful servants, that their endeavours to win new disciples for Christ may be fruitful. Those who oppose them will be unsuccessful.

...the synagogue of Satan (Revelation 3:9)

There is no word of condemnation to this missionary church. Many of the city's Jewish population were won over by the missionary activity of this church with the consequence that they faced opposition from those in the city who called themselves Jews, but who were proved to be *of the synagogue of Satan (Revelation 3:9)* by their actions. These were Jews who blasphemed Christ and rejected Him as the Messiah. Those in the *synagogue of Satan* will, at the end of this [4]church age, worship before the feet of these saints that they so vehemently opposed. The Lord confirms His pleasure in this church by reminding them that He will remove them from the world before the time of [5]tribulation upon the earth (Revelation 3:10). Those so removed will be identified as God's own, will be destined for the heavenly city, New Jerusalem, and will be given a new name (Revelation 3:12). The *'name of my God'*, *'the name of the city of my God'* and the Christian's *'new name'* will be <u>written</u> on him, signifying that his new position is absolutely permanent.

Laodicea (Revelation 3:14-22)

A wealthy city located near Colossae (Colossians 4:13-16) and about 40 miles from Ephesus. This city's wealth was so great that in AD 60, when it was almost completely destroyed by an earthquake, its citizens refused Rome's aid and rebuilt the city at their own expense. As an industrial centre it was known for the production of fine black wool, and for its Phrygian powder, used to treat eye diseases. Hot mineral springs made it a medical centre as well.

The Lord Jesus Christ describes himself as *the Amen, the faithful and true witness, the beginning of the creation of God*. The literal

---

[4]The period in history commencing from the Ascension of Christ (Mark 16:19) until His return in glory to remove His church from the world (1 Cor 15:50-54, 1 Thess 4:13-17, 2 Thess 2:7).

[5]This is the final seven years on the earth during which the earth will be in great trouble. This is the 70th week in Daniel chapter 9:27. It is covered in the book of Revelation from the 6th to 19th chapters and will be covered in detail later in the book.

translation of *the Amen* is 'the steadfast one'. Christ's description of Himself is a direct contrast to the way that He describes them.

And unto the angel of the church of the Laodiceans write; These things saith the Amen, the faithful and true witness, the beginning of the creation of God; I know thy works, that thou art neither cold nor hot: I would thou wert cold or hot. So then because thou art lukewarm, and neither cold nor hot, I will spue thee out of my mouth. Because thou sayest, I am rich, and increased with goods, and have need of nothing; and knowest not that thou art wretched, and miserable, and poor, and blind, and naked: I counsel thee to buy of me gold tried in the fire, that thou mayest be rich; and white raiment, that thou mayest be clothed, and that the shame of thy nakedness do not appear; and anoint thine eyes with eyesalve, that thou mayest see. As many as I love, I rebuke and chasten: be zealous therefore, and repent. Behold, I stand at the door, and knock: if any man hear my voice, and open the door, I will come in to him, and will sup with him, and he with me. To him that overcometh will I grant to sit with me in my throne, even as I also overcame, and am set down with my Father in his throne. He that hath an ear, let him hear what the Spirit saith unto the churches. (Revelation 3:14-22)

thou art neither cold nor hot (Revelation 3:15)

This is the only church for which the Lord has no word of commendation. What is their sin? They are accused of being *neither cold nor hot*, just lukewarm. They had at one time accepted Christ as Lord and Saviour, but they had drifted away from Him and now were Christian in name only. They were not enthusiastic about the things of God, but at the same time they did not deny Him. That they were Christians is evident from the address on their letter – *the <u>church</u> of the Laodiceans (Revelation 3:14)*. Their meeting as a church group was just religious observance, and Christ found their lukewarm state nauseating; He says *because thou art lukewarm, and neither cold nor hot, I will spue thee out of my mouth (Revelation 3:16)* – an apt expression for a renowned medical centre.

thou sayest, I am rich, ...and knowest not that thou art wretched, and miserable, and poor, and blind, and naked (Revelation 3:17)

Laodicea was a very wealthy city, but Christ describes them as *poor*. It was famed for the high quality of the wool it produced, used only in the finest clothing, but Christ describes them as *naked*. It was also known for its production of a powder used to treat eye diseases; the Lord, however, describes them as *blind*. How very appropriate was the Lord's description of their spiritual state. They said *I am rich, and increased with goods, and have need of nothing* but Christ said *thou art wretched, and miserable, and poor, and blind, and naked*. Their spiritual condition was the exact opposite of their physical condition.

I counsel thee to buy of me gold tried in the fire... (Revelation 3:18)

The Apostle Paul wrote on this subject in 1 Corinthians chapter 3:

...other foundation can no man lay than that is laid, which is Jesus Christ. Now if any man build upon this foundation gold, silver, precious stones, wood, hay, stubble; Every man's work shall be made manifest: for the day shall declare it, because it shall be revealed by fire; and the fire shall try every man's work of what sort it is. If any man's work abide which he hath built thereupon, he shall receive a reward. If any man's work shall be burned, he shall suffer loss: but he himself shall be saved; yet so as by fire. (1 Cor 3:11-15)

From the description of the Laodiceans, I don't think they had anything in the way of *gold*; but they had plenty of *wood, hay, stubble*. This is not referring to physical riches, but spiritual riches

48

– the character of the church; the character of individual
Christians, their works, their attitudes, their love and devotion to
the Lord Jesus Christ, to each other, and to those around them.
These were the riches that Paul was writing to the Corinthians
about. These were the riches that the Lord Jesus Christ wanted the
Laodiceans to have, and He wanted them to strive for the very
best in spiritual riches – <u>gold</u> – and not just any gold either!
Unrefined gold contains impurities. When the gold is heated to
melting point, the impurities rise to the surface as dross which can
then be skimmed off. The Lord Himself is the refiner of our
spiritual gold. He is the one who removes the dross from our
lives; those things which Paul described as *wood, hay, stubble*. He
is the one who 'tries us by fire', and burns up the things in our
lives that are contrary to His nature. The gold that the Lord
wanted for the Laodiceans was pure gold that had been *tried in
the fire (Revelation 3:18)*. Pure gold is very valuable, and very
expensive. The purer the gold is, the softer and more malleable it
is. The Lord wanted the Laodiceans to be like pure gold that He
could easily craft to be more like Himself.

How were the Laodiceans to get this gold?

How could a lukewarm church obtain such spiritual riches, even
gold in its raw state for the Lord to refine? Was He going to
give it to them and then refine it? No, verse 18 says that they
were to <u>buy</u> it from Him. How much was it going to cost them?
Pure gold is very expensive; how much it costs depends on the
individual: Jesus told the rich man in Matthew 19:21 *...sell what
thou hast, and give to the poor, and thou shalt have treasure in
heaven: and come and follow me*. The price was too high for
this man and *he went away sorrowful: for he had great
possessions (Mt 19:22)*. For some the price might be to be sent
into the world as a Missionary, as in Mark 10:28-30 where Peter
said to the Lord *...we have left all and have followed thee. And
Jesus answered and said, Verily I say unto you, There is no man*

that hath left house, or brethren, or sisters, or father, or mother, or wife, or children, or lands, for my sake, and the gospel's, but he shall receive an hundredfold now in this time, houses, and brethren, and sisters, and mothers, and children, and lands, with persecutions; and in the world to come eternal life. [6]For others it might cost their life, just as it cost Stephen his life, [7]or it might mean the life of a Pastor; we have in scripture the Pastorship of Timothy at Ephesus. The cost is not what <u>you</u> would like to do for the Lord, it is what the Lord would have you to do for Him. He did not say to the rich man 'what would you like to do?', He <u>told</u> him to *sell what you have, ... and ... follow me.* The same was going to apply to the Laodiceans. He said in Revelation 3:18 *I <u>counsel</u> thee to buy of me gold tried in the fire.* The Lord Himself was their counsellor and was going to instruct them as to the cost of His gold.

Behold, I stand at the door and knock... (Revelation 3:20)

A fuller understanding of this verse can be gained by consideration of the customs of the land:

1) When someone knocked at the door, it would not be opened immediately. The one inside would talk with the one who knocked through the closed door to try to recognise his voice and identify him as a friend.
Acts 12:13-14 says *And as Peter knocked at the door of the gate, a damsel came to hearken, named Rhoda. And when she knew Peter's voice, she opened not the gate for gladness.*

---

[6]Acts 6:8 to 8:2

[7]See the book of 1 Timothy

2) [8]When a guest was entertained he was regarded as the lord or master of the house.

3) When the host shared a meal with the guest, it was like taking a vow of allegiance; subsequent shared meals would renew that covenant. They would not eat the food of their enemies, or of people who were hostile to their cause. This is why Abraham's servant would not eat the food of Laban until he had first declared his task of finding a wife for Isaac (Gen 24:33).

Application of this in Revelation 3:20:

1) We should not open the door of our heart to just anyone who knocks; we must first recognise the voice of Christ before opening that door.

2) When we open the door, Christ (the guest) should become our Lord and Master.

3) Because He sups with us and we with him (see Revelation 3:20), we swear our allegiance to Him and He makes a covenant with us, i.e.:

   1 Corinthians 11:25 ...*This cup is the new testament* [or covenant] *in my blood* – through this covenant we have forgiveness of sins and eternal life when we accept Him as our Lord (John 3:14-18).

---

[8]See Genesis 19:1-3

It is an everlasting covenant – Hebrews 13:5 *I will never leave thee, nor forsake thee.*

4

Revelation chapter 4:
'Thou art worthy, O Lord'

Chapters 4 and 5 of Revelation take us from the past, portrayed
in the letters to the seven churches, into the present, and prepare
us for the future – the opening of the seven seals of God's
Judgement upon the earth, which starts in Revelation chapter
six. Three of these seals have already been opened. This is
prophecy fulfilled! More of this later when we look specifically
at that portion of Revelation.

*After this I looked, and, behold, a door was opened in heaven:
and the first voice which I heard was as it were of a trumpet
talking with me; which said, Come up hither, and I will shew thee
things which must be hereafter. And immediately I was in the
spirit: and, behold, a throne was set in heaven, and one sat on the
throne. And he that sat was to look upon like a jasper and a
sardine stone: and there was a rainbow round about the throne,
in sight like unto an emerald. And round about the throne were
four and twenty seats: and upon the seats I saw four and twenty
elders sitting, clothed in white raiment; and they had on their
heads crowns of gold. And out of the throne proceeded lightnings
and thunderings and voices: and there were seven lamps of fire
burning before the throne, which are the seven Spirits of God.
And before the throne there was a sea of glass like unto crystal:
and in the midst of the throne, and round about the throne, were
four beasts full of eyes before and behind. And the first beast was
like a lion, and the second beast like a calf, and the third beast
had a face as a man, and the fourth beast was like a flying eagle.
And the four beasts had each of them six wings about him; and*

*they were full of eyes within: and they rest not day and night,
saying, Holy, holy, holy, Lord God Almighty, which was, and is,
and is to come. And when those beasts give glory and honour and
thanks to him that sat on the throne, who liveth for ever and ever,
The four and twenty elders fall down before him that sat on the
throne, and worship him that liveth for ever and ever, and cast
their crowns before the throne, saying, Thou art worthy, O Lord,
to receive glory and honour and power: for thou hast created all
things, and for thy pleasure they are and were created.
(Revelation 4:1-11)*

After this...a door was opened in heaven (Revelation 4:1)

John, in his vision, saw a door opened in Heaven, and again he
heard that voice like a trumpet talking with him. [1] The voice of
the Lord Jesus Christ, which said *Come up hither, and I will
shew thee things which must be hereafter (Revelation 4:1).*
John, in his vision, was caught up into Heaven, and beheld such
an awesome sight that he struggled to find adequate words to
describe the things which he saw. It is said that a picture is
worth a thousand words. However I have yet to see a painting
that can do justice to this scene. If you let your imagination
paint the picture in your mind, you get a glimpse of this scene
that just cannot be put down on paper.

And he that sat was to look upon like a jasper and a sardine stone (Revelation 4:3)

John saw a throne and someone sitting on that throne. *And he
that sat was to look upon like a jasper and a sardine stone
(Revelation 4:3).* In Exodus chapter 28, instructions are given

---

[1] Compare Revelation 1:10

for making the high priest's breastplate. In Exodus 28:17, the first stone to be mounted in the high priest's breastplate was a sardius, and in Exodus 28:20, the last stone is a jasper. So the description in Revelation indicates that the one sitting on the throne is the Lord Jesus Christ, our Great High Priest, the Alpha and Omega, the first and the last, which is exactly the way the Lord Jesus Christ describes Himself in chapter 1. However when we come to Revelation 5:6-7, the Lamb (i.e. Christ) *took the book out of the right hand of him that sat upon the throne*, which seems to indicate that it is the Father upon the throne. Revelation 3:21 may shed some light on this conundrum; Christ says ...*I also overcame, and am set down with my Father in His throne*. It would seem that the Father and the Son are both upon the heavenly throne.

there was a rainbow round about the throne, in sight like an emerald (Revelation 4:3)

The emerald was used as the seal in a signet ring. [2]The rainbow is God's sign that He will never again destroy the earth by a flood. There is now a seal on this promise; despite the terrible judgements to come at the opening of the seven seals of judgement, God reaffirms that He will not destroy the earth with a flood.

The 24 elders in verse 4 are probably the 12 Apostles and the leaders of the 12 tribes of Israel. Texts supporting this view are:

- Revelation 21:14, where we are told concerning the heavenly city, New Jerusalem, that *the wall of the city had twelve foundations, and in them the names of the twelve apostles of the Lamb*.

---

[2]Genesis 8:20-22, Genesis 9:11-17

- In Revelation 7:4-8 and Revelation 14:1, we read of 144,000 Jews redeemed during the tribulation period, 12,000 from each of the 12 tribes of Israel.

- In Revelation 21:12, we are told that New Jerusalem had 12 gates *and at the gates twelve angels, and names written thereon, which are the names of the twelve tribes of the children of Israel.*

These elders are all clothed with white raiment. Revelation 19:8 tells us that white raiment is the righteousness of saints. *...and they had on their heads crowns of gold.* Crowns in the New Testament are rewards for the faithful.

...the seven Spirits of God (Revelation 4:5)

For an explanation of the term *the seven Spirits of God (Revelation 4:5)*, see chapter one: 'Why are there seven Spirits? (Revelation 1:4)'.

before the throne there was a sea of glass like unto crystal (Revelation 4:6)

The *sea of glass* is a very comforting illustration of what Heaven holds for the believer. The *sea* has the same symbolic meaning here as in Revelation chapter 13:1 where John said he *saw a beast rise up out of the sea.* The sea, is a sea of nations: in Revelation 13:1 the Beast comes to power in the world: he rises up out of the nations of the world. Isaiah uses the same symbolism in Isaiah 57:20, *the wicked are like the troubled sea, when it cannot rest, whose waters cast up mire and dirt.* The sea, like the nations, never rests; it is always searching, always striving, always on the move. But in Revelation 4:6, in contrast to the troubled sea, denoting the turmoil of nations striving against one another, the sea is glass, the striving is over, no more political turmoil, no more upheaval, no more uncertainty. It is literally a sea of tranquillity with Christ on the throne before it.

in the midst of the throne, and round about the throne, were four beasts full of eyes before and behind (Revelation 4:6)

We are now introduced to four beasts, who are in the midst and round about the throne. We are not told what these four beasts are. Their appearance is similar to, but not exactly like that of the four living creatures that [3]Ezekiel describes in his vision. If you compare Ezekiel chapter 1 with Revelation chapter 4, there are so many similarities, that the slight differences are probably due to their being described by different authors. In Ezekiel chapter 10 we are told that those which Ezekiel saw were cherubim, which are symbolic of God's [4]holy presence and glory, and [5]guardians of God's righteousness and mercy. Considering the remarkable similarities in the two accounts, there can be little doubt that the four beasts in Revelation are cherubim. We are told in Revelation 4:7 that one beast was like a lion, the second like a calf, the third had a face like a man, and the fourth was like a flying eagle. These likenesses symbolise qualities of the Lord Jesus Christ:

The lion is symbolic of Christ's majesty. He is the Lord of lords and the King of kings (Revelation 17:14).

---

[3]Ezekiel 1:4-14

[4]Revelation 4:8

[5]Genesis 3:24, Exodus 25:17-22

The calf is symbolic of Christ's sacrifice. We usually think of His sacrifice in terms like [6]*the lamb of God* but here the symbolism is that of a calf. Two interesting scriptures came to light as I pondered the meaning of this verse:

Hosea 14:2 ...*turn to the LORD: say unto him, Take away all iniquity, and receive us graciously: so will we render the calves* [i.e. sacrifice] *of our lips.*

Hebrews 13:15 *By him therefore let us offer the sacrifice of praise to God continually, that is, the fruit of our lips giving thanks to his name.*

The face of a man refers to Christ's humanity. Although He was the Son of God, the Lord Jesus Christ loved to describe Himself as the [7]Son of man. He lived on this earth for over 30 years but [8]never once sinned in any way. [9]His ultimate work was to die on the cross at Calvary as the perfect sacrifice that was required to reconcile us to God.

The flying eagle is symbolic of Christ's victory at [10]Armageddon. The 'eagle' is flying high, ready to swoop on its prey, and will swiftly conquer the Beast and his armies. Matthew 24:27-28 says *For as the lightning cometh out of the east, and shineth even unto the west: so shall also the coming of the Son of man be. For wheresoever the carcase is, there will*

---

[6]e.g. John 1:29, 36

[7]e.g. Matthew 8:20

[8]Hebrews 4:14-15

[9]Hebrews 9:24-28

[10]Revelation 19:11-21

the eagles be gathered together. The spiritual implication is that where moral corruption exists, divine judgement falls. The corruption and degeneration of the world under the command of the Beast will be swiftly countered by the judgement of God. The world will degenerate so fast under the Beast's rule when the Holy Spirit is [11]removed from the world that God will only allow it to continue for seven years before putting an end to it.

The scene in chapter 4 ends with heavenly praise from the cherubim and worship from the 24 elders. The object of their adoration is the One seated upon the throne.

---

[11] 1 Cor 15:50-54, 1 Thess 4:13-17, 2 Thess 2:7

5

Revelation chapter 5:
The seven sealed book

And I saw in the right hand of him that sat on the throne a book written within and on the backside, sealed with seven seals. And I saw a strong angel proclaiming with a loud voice, Who is worthy to open the book, and to loose the seals thereof? And no man in heaven, nor in earth, neither under the earth, was able to open the book, neither to look thereon. And I wept much, because no man was found worthy to open and to read the book, neither to look thereon. And one of the elders saith unto me, Weep not: behold, the Lion of the tribe of Juda, the Root of David, hath prevailed to open the book, and to loose the seven seals thereof. And I beheld, and, lo, in the midst of the throne and of the four beasts, and in the midst of the elders, stood a Lamb as it had been slain, having seven horns and seven eyes, which are the seven Spirits of God sent forth into all the earth. (Revelation 5:1-6)

The seven sealed book—this would actually have been a scroll—contains the full account of God's intended judgements on the world. It is sealed with seven seals indicating that it is complete. It has been declared to us by the Lord Jesus Christ and is therefore now unchangeable. The events signified by the opening of the seven seals are inevitable.

This is the position of Christians too, as children of God: Ephesians 1:13-14 says, *In* [Christ] *ye also trusted, after that ye heard the word of truth, the gospel of your salvation: in whom also after that ye believed, ye were **sealed** with that Holy Spirit of promise, which is the earnest of our inheritance* *until the redemption of the purchased possession, unto the praise of his glory.*

So when we believe we are **sealed** with the Holy Spirit. In the olden days when documents or letters were sealed with wax and the signet impression was pressed into the wax, it meant that:

1) The document was complete, the work was finished.

2) The signet impression showed who the owner was.

So when we are sealed by God, the signet impression is the Holy Spirit Himself, therefore we are God's possession. The fact that we are sealed indicates a finished work (we are redeemed by the blood of Christ – He has paid the price of our sin). We remain sealed until *the redemption of the purchased possession (Eph 1:14)*. So because that seal remains unbroken we have security of salvation.

The scroll is written on both sides and bound with seven seals. [1]The number seven is a number of divine completeness. The fact that there are seven seals symbolises the completeness of the sealing, until one qualified to loose the seals and open the scroll should appear (Revelation 5:2-5). The seals are probably arranged such that as each one is broken, a portion of the scroll can be unrolled and read.

---

[1]God rested on the seventh day (Gen 2:2-3), and commands us to do likewise (Ex 20:8-11), see also Ex 25:37, Deut 28:25, Proverbs 26:16, Is 4:1, Is 11:15, Mk 16:9, and in the book of Revelation: 1:12, 5:6, 8:2, 10:3, 15:1, 17:1

...in the midst of the throne...stood a Lamb as it had been slain, having seven horns... (Revelation 5:6)

It has already been mentioned that seven is the number of divine completeness. [2]The horn is symbolic of power, honour and authority. This [3]Lamb (i.e. Christ) has seven horns, therefore the symbolism is complete and all the attributes in Revelation 5:12 are appropriate. Power, because He has [4]conquered death, not just for Himself but for all who believe. Honour and authority, because He is now *sat down on the right hand of the majesty on high (Heb 1:3).*

And he came and took the book out of the right hand of him that sat upon the throne. And when he had taken the book, the four beasts and four and twenty elders fell down before the Lamb, having every one of them harps, and golden vials full of odours, which are the prayers of saints. And they sung a new song, saying, Thou art worthy to take the book, and to open the seals thereof: for thou wast slain, and hast redeemed us to God by thy blood out of every kindred, and tongue, and people, and nation; And hast made us unto our God kings and priests: and we shall reign on the earth. And I beheld, and I heard the voice of many angels round about the throne and the beasts and the elders: and the number of them was ten thousand times ten thousand, and thousands of thousands; Saying with a loud voice, Worthy is the

---

[2]The following scriptures are examples of the symbolism behind the term 'horn'. I have split them up into groups but you will notice that some of them signify more than one attribute. The horn of power: Deut 33:17, 1 Kings 22:11. The horn of honour: Job 16:15, Lamentations 2:3. The horn of authority: Dan 2:1-12, Zechariah 1:18-21.

[3]John 1:29, 1 Peter 1:18-19

[4]John 3:16, 1 Cor.15:54-55

Lamb that was slain to receive power, and riches, and wisdom, and strength, and honour, and glory, and blessing. And every creature which is in heaven, and on the earth, and under the earth, and such as are in the sea, and all that are in them, heard I saying, Blessing, and honour, and glory, and power, be unto him that sitteth upon the throne, and unto the Lamb for ever and ever. And the four beasts said, Amen. And the four and twenty elders fell down and worshipped him that liveth for ever and ever. (Revelation 5:7-14)

The Lord Jesus Christ is the only one who is worthy to open the scroll because He is pure. There is no fault in Him whatsoever. He is sinless and He has paid the price of our salvation with His own blood (Revelation 5:9); therefore He alone is worthy to open the scroll.

What was the result in Heaven of Christ taking the scroll? (Revelation 5:7)

When the Lord Jesus Christ took the scroll, John, in his vision saw all in Heaven and earth rejoice and worship the Lord. Prayer and worship are synonymous with the Old Testament practice of offering of [5] incense; hence Revelation 5:8: *And when he had taken the book, the four beasts and four and twenty elders fell down before the Lamb, having every one of them harps, and golden vials full of odours, which are the prayers of saints.*

---

[5] e.g. Malachi 1:11, Revelation 5:8, Revelation 8:3

64

6

Revelation chapter 6:
Six seals of judgement

In Revelation chapter six, we read about six of the seven seals of God's judgements upon the inhabitants of the earth. The seals are warnings of judgements to come. There have been glimpses of these judgements ever since Adam and Eve sinned, but God delayed the start of the actual judgements until the time of this revelation to John. The warning signs can be seen right back to the time of Adam and Eve but the actual judgements were delayed until the time was right.

[1]In time past, God warned the Israelites of the consequences of their disobedience and when they sinned the threat was carried out. [2]On occasions God's judgement was averted by the supplication of Moses – a godly man. This shows just how important it is for Christians to continue praying for revival, even in this wayward generation. Many of the warnings in this portion of Revelation are similar to those that Israel were warned of. [3]The difference is that in Revelation, God is not just warning Israel, He is warning the whole world. In Genesis 15:16, God's judgement upon the Amorites was

---

[1] e.g. Jeremiah 25:1-12 (with 2 Kings chapters 22 to 25 and Daniel 1:1-2).

[2] e.g. Exodus 32:1-14

[3] Those who believe are the children of God, His chosen people are now not just the nation of Israel, but all nations are included. See Galatians 3:6-9, 13-16, 28-29.

delayed for 400 years because He said ...*the iniquity of the Amorites is not yet full.* So it is with these judgements in Revelation. God is waiting for the right time to unleash His judgements upon the earth. We see another aspect of God's judgement too in His judgement upon the great Assyrian city of Nineveh. [4]In the book of Jonah, God declared that Nineveh would be overthrown in 40 days time, but because Nineveh repented, God delayed His judgement for about 150 years, when as prophesied by Nahum, Nineveh was conquered in 612 BC by the Medes and Chaldeans. So it is with God's judgements upon the earth in Revelation; although there is no specific time declared for it, it is certain to happen because God has said so, but it can be delayed if people take heed of the warnings and turn to God in repentance.

Mankind cannot afford to be complacent; these are not judgements that are far off in the distant future. They have already started! Three of these seals have already been opened! It is only the genuine repentance of mankind that can delay the remainder of these judgements. As a nation we have strayed very far from God. The rules that God has provided us with for peace and prosperity are constantly being overturned by people who think they know better than God. As an example, our leaders have relaxed the Sunday trading laws – do they really know better than God who said [5]*Remember the sabbath day, to*

---

[4]Jonah 3:1-5

[5]Exodus 20:8-11. There is much confusion about which day is the sabbath in this country. In Israel, Saturday is the sabbath, their day of rest, and rightly so in their culture which is very different to our own. On many of our calendars, Sunday is shown as the first day of the week, and Saturday as the seventh. This is very misleading: consider the layout of the week in this country. Our working week starts with Monday and the sixth working day is therefore Saturday.
Exodus 20:9-10 makes it very clear which day is the sabbath; it is the day after

keep it holy. Six days shalt thou labour, and do all thy work: But the seventh day is the sabbath of the LORD thy God, in it thou shalt not do any work, thou, nor thy son, nor thy daughter, thy manservant, nor thy maidservant, nor thy cattle, nor thy stranger that is within thy gates: For in six days the LORD made heaven and earth, the sea and all that in them is, and rested the seventh day: wherefore the LORD blessed the sabbath day, and hallowed it (Exodus 20:8-11).

The times when God's punishment toward Israel was averted by the supplication of Moses were not prophetic judgements. The judgements foretold in Revelation are (obviously) prophetic and therefore inevitable. They will definitely happen; however they can, and should, be delayed if it is possible. After all, death is inevitable, but we do not resign ourselves to die every time we get sick; we do what is necessary for recovery and to delay the hand of death. I wonder how many times God has delayed His wrath from this nation because of the prayer of His saints, or because of the repentance of our nation during times of revival?

The first four seals – the four horses and their riders (Revelation 6:1-8)

These four horses and their riders are symbolic of events on the earth. The intensity of these judgements will increase dramatically towards the end of this age.

The **WHITE** horse symbolises **FALSE CHRISTS** or **FALSE MESSIAHS**.

The **RED** horse symbolises **WAR**.

---

the six working days of the week. Therefore Sunday is the sabbath in this country and should be shown as the last day of the week on our calendars.

The **BLACK** horse symbolises **FAMINE**.

The **PALE** horse symbolises **DEATH**.

The Lord Jesus Christ warned His disciples of these things in
Matthew 24:3-8. It is well worth taking the time to read the
whole chapter. Christ warns of:

- False Christs (Matthew 24:4-5)

- Wars and rumours of wars (Matthew 24:6-7)

- Famines (Matthew 24:7)

- Other aspects concerning the end of the age
  (Matthew 24:8 onward)

False Christs, wars, famines and death seem to come in 'waves'.
They are not increasing constantly. In Matthew 24:8, Jesus says,
All these are the beginning of sorrows. The word *sorrow* has the
meaning of a woman in labour, giving birth to a child. There are
lulls when God's judgement seems to be suspended; these may
be times of revival. Then, as people move away from God,
perhaps generations later, the judgements are again apparent
and there is another 'wave'. As with childbirth, these 'waves'
will increase in frequency and intensity until eventually God's
full judgement is unleashed upon the earth.

The first seal – the white horse – false messiahs (Revelation 6:1-2)

*And I saw when the Lamb opened one of the seals, and I heard,
as it were the noise of thunder, one of the four beasts saying,
Come and see. And I saw, and behold a white horse: and he that*

sat on him had a bow; and a crown was given unto him: and he went forth conquering, and to conquer. (Revelation 6:1-2)

...many shall come in my name, saying, I am Christ; and shall deceive many (Matthew 24:5)

Every now and then we hear of someone who claims to be the Messiah. These false Christs pave the way for the ultimate false Christ – the one the Bible calls the Antichrist. Each false Messiah hardens hearts against the Lord Jesus Christ and softens up the way for the revelation of the true Antichrist. This Antichrist is also known as the *beast*. We read about him with this name in Revelation chapter 13. In Daniel 9:26 he is called *the prince that shall come*. Another name that he has is *the man of sin* or *the son of perdition*, names that we find in 2 Thessalonians chapter 2; a chapter that reveals a great deal about this man and the time in which he is revealed for who he is. 2 Thess 2:3-4 says that the day of Christ *shall not come, except there come a falling away first, and that man of sin be revealed, the son of perdition; who opposeth and exalteth himself above all that is called God, or that is worshipped; so that he as God sitteth in the temple of God, shewing himself that he is God.* This man will imitate Christ; many have imitated Christ before and have demanded worship, but this man will sit in the temple of God in Jerusalem, claiming to be God and demand worship. [6]He will receive it too, on a scale never seen before, on penalty of death.

His rule on earth will not start this way though. [7]Initially he will seem to be the patron of the Jews. He will make a covenant with

---

[6]Revelation 13:4, 12-17

[7]Dan 9:27

them, allowing them to resume temple worship and sacrifice according to the Old Testament laws. After 3½ years however he will renounce the covenant and will seat himself in the temple, claim to be God and demand worship. This is the start of the Great Tribulation. This is the time that the Lord Jesus Christ referred to when He said in Matthew 24:15-22, *When ye therefore shall see the abomination of desolation spoken of by Daniel the prophet, stand in the holy place, (whoso readeth, let him understand:) then let them which be in Judaea flee into the mountains: Let him which is on the housetop not come down to take anything out of his house: Neither let him which is in the field return back to take his clothes. And woe unto them that are with child, and to them that give suck in those days! But pray ye that your flight be not in the winter, neither on the sabbath day: For then shall be great tribulation, such as was not since the beginning of the world to this time, no nor ever shall be. And except those days should be shortened, there should no flesh be saved: but for the elect's sake those days shall be shortened.*

Let us turn now to the book of Daniel and learn more of this man:

In Daniel 2:1, Nebuchadnezzar, king of Babylon had a dream: *And in the second year of the reign of Nebuchadnezzar, Nebuchadnezzar dreamed dreams, wherewith his spirit was troubled, and his sleep brake from him.*

Daniel was called to reveal the dream and its interpretation to the king; in Daniel 2:31-45, Daniel says: *Thou, O king, sawest, and behold a great image. This great image, whose brightness was excellent, stood before thee; and the form thereof was terrible. This image's head was of fine gold, his breast and his arms of silver, his belly and his thighs of brass, his legs of iron, his feet part of iron and part of clay. Thou sawest till that a stone was cut out without hands, which smote the image upon his feet that were of iron and clay, and brake them to pieces.*

Then was the iron, the clay, the brass, the silver, and the gold, broken to pieces together, and became like the chaff of the summer threshing-floors; and the wind carried them away, that no place was found for them: and the stone that smote the image became a great mountain, and filled the whole earth.

This is the dream; and we will tell the interpretation thereof before the king.

Thou, O king, art a king of kings: for the God of heaven hath given thee a kingdom, power, and strength, and glory. And wheresoever the children of men dwell, the beasts of the field and the fowls of the heaven hath he given into thine hand, and hath made thee ruler over them all. Thou art this head of gold. And after thee shall arise another kingdom inferior to thee, and another third kingdom of brass, which shall bear rule over all the earth. And the fourth kingdom shall be strong as iron: forasmuch as iron breaketh in pieces and subdueth all things: and as iron that breaketh all these, shall it break in pieces and bruise. And whereas thou sawest the feet and toes, part of potter's clay, and part of iron, the kingdom shall be divided; but there shall be in it of the strength of the iron, forasmuch as thou sawest the iron mixed with miry clay. And as the toes of the feet were part of iron, and part of clay, so the kingdom shall be partly strong, and partly broken. And whereas thou sawest iron mixed with miry clay, they shall mingle themselves with the seed of men: but they shall not cleave one to another, even as iron is not mixed with clay. And in the days of these kings shall the God of heaven set up a kingdom, which shall never be destroyed: and the kingdom shall not be left to other people, but it shall break in pieces and consume all these kingdoms, and it shall stand for ever. Forasmuch as thou sawest that the stone was cut out of the mountain without hands, and that it brake in pieces the iron, the brass, the clay, the silver, and the gold; the great God hath made known to the king what shall come to pass hereafter: and the dream is certain, and the interpretation thereof sure.

The image was an object lesson portraying the history of the Gentile nations from the time of Nebuchadnezzar until the second coming of Christ. Nebuchadnezzar's dream was a prophecy of the four world empires, starting with his own, the head of gold, representing the Babylonian empire which then had control over the Jews and their land.

Following the Babylonian empire came another empire represented by the breast and arms of silver. In 538 BC, Darius the Mede moved in with his armies and conquered the Babylonians. Then the Medes united with the Persians to form the second world empire of the [8]Medes and Persians, and for some time this kingdom ruled over Israel and the Jewish people.

The third world power is symbolised by the belly and thighs of brass representing the Grecian empire headed by Alexander the Great (Greek-Macedonian empire).

The fourth world empire, that of the Romans, is characterised by the legs of iron. This empire continued for some time, eventually being divided into two parts: east and west, represented by the two legs (vs 33). One section had Rome as its capital and the other Constantinople. The Roman empire disintegrated as a world power, but has remained through the centuries in fragmentary form. In other words the countries which made up the Roman empire became independent powers (Italy, Germany, Britain, etc.) However, in the last days (the days immediately prior to the second coming of Jesus Christ), the Roman empire is going to be revived in a

---

[8]We know this from history, but see also Dan 5:31

new form, symbolised by the ten toes of the image
(Dan 2:42). This last form of Gentile power will be a coalition
of ten nations from the area of the old Roman empire (the ten
nations are also represented by the ten horns of Dan 7:7 and
Revelation 13:1). These nations will choose a leader who will,
through this coalition, get control of the whole world
(Revelation 13:7-8). This leader is the Antichrist, the Beast,
the son of perdition, the man of sin, the prince that shall come.
During his [9]seven year reign the world will be brought to
complete ruin (5th, 6th, and 7th seals).

The second seal – the red horse – war (Revelation 6:3-4)

*And when he had opened the second seal, I heard the second
beast say, Come and see. And there went out another horse that
was red: and power was given to him that sat thereon to take
peace from the earth, and that they should kill one another: and
there was given unto him a great sword. (Revelation 6:3-4)*

*...ye shall hear of wars and rumours of wars... for nation shall
rise against nation, and kingdom against kingdom
(Matthew 24:6-7)*

The rule of the Beast, or the Antichrist, will ultimately lead to the
[10]battle of Armageddon where the Lord Jesus Christ and His
heavenly army will destroy the armies of the Beast. Without
Christ's intervention in this way, mankind under the Beast's rule

---

[9]Daniel 9:27 (the word *week* in Daniel 9:27, literally means 'a seven' or
'a week'. Its meaning here is 'a week of years'. It is also used in this sense in
Genesis 29:27 *Fulfil her week... yet seven other years*

[10] Revelation chapters 16 and 19

would destroy each other completely. Jesus told His disciples in Matthew 24:22, ...*except those days* (the tribulation period, i.e. the Beast's rule) *should be shortened, there should no flesh be saved: but for the [11]elect's sake those days shall be shortened.* The power behind the Beast is Satan, [12]the god of this world system, and as long as he is free in the world, wars will continue.

In the context of ever increasing warfare, Jesus said in Matthew 24:6 ...*see that ye be not troubled: for all these things must come to pass, but the end is not yet.* War is unavoidable. In a nuclear war, it is estimated by man that a quarter of the world population would be killed. The Bible says that <u>all</u> mankind would be killed, not just a third! Nuclear war would be certain under the rule of the Beast but for one thing – Christ's intervention! It is clear from Matthew 24:22 that if the Beast's rule were allowed to continue unchecked, the result would be complete annihilation for mankind – *And except those days should be shortened, there should <u>no flesh be saved</u>: but for the elect's sake those days shall be shortened.*

The third seal – the black horse – famine and disease (Revelation 6:5-6)

And when he had opened the third seal, I heard the third beast say, Come and see. And I beheld, and lo a black horse; and he that sat on him had a pair of balances in his hand. And I heard a voice in the midst of the four beasts say, A measure of wheat for a

---

[11] The elect referred to here are those who come to believe in the Lord Jesus Christ during the tribulation period.

[12] 2 Corinthians 4:4, John 12:31

*penny, and three measures of barley for a penny; and see thou
hurt not the oil and the wine. (Revelation 6:5-6)*

*...nation shall rise against nation, and kingdom against kingdom:
and there shall be famines, and pestilences, and earthquakes, in
divers* [diverse] *places. (Matthew 24:7)*

The amount of money translated in the Authorized Version of
the Bible as *a penny*, was a day's wages for a labourer in John's
day. What this verse says is that a day's wages will buy one
measure of wheat, or three measures of barley. A whole day's
wages will only buy enough of the cheapest grain for three
small meals for one person. When there is famine there is
rampant inflation!

...and do not harm the oil and the wine. This indicates that
famine will coexist with luxury.

The rider on the black horse indicates that <u>false religion</u> (white
horse) <u>leads to war</u> (red horse) and that <u>war leads to famine</u> (in
Matthew 24:7, Jesus links famine with disease). Following the
white and red horses, famine will prevail upon the earth. Jesus
told His disciples that famine would starve whole peoples in
various parts of the world; *...nation shall rise against nation,
and kingdom against kingdom: and there shall be famines, and
pestilences, and earthquakes, in divers* [diverse] *places
(Matthew 24:7).* In other parts of the world though there would
be those who live in luxury, i.e. Matthew 24:37-39, *But as the
days of Noe* [Noah] *were, so shall also the coming of the Son of
man be. For as in the days that were before the flood they were
eating and drinking, marrying and giving in marriage, until the
day that Noe entered into the ark. And knew not until the flood
came, and took them all away; so shall also the coming of the
Son of man be.*

The connection between these two passages is simply that in both cases the Lord is speaking of the same time; the time leading up to His second coming and of the end of this age. These two conditions: poverty/famine and riches/luxury will be parallel and simultaneous. We can see it in the world today but it will become much more so as we near the end of the age. The Bible says that a man will work a whole day just to feed himself and there will be nothing left over for his family to eat, while others will live in luxury.

Man's answer to the world's problems will be a world government, headed by the Beast, or the Antichrist. He will attempt to answer the problems of the world and will fail, but [13]Christ's future kingdom when He reigns here on earth for 1000 years will solve the world's problems. It is a foregone conclusion that a man-made world government will fail because it is directly against God's will. [14]It is clear from Genesis chapter 11 that we are supposed to exist as separate countries under individual rule. Man is incapable of a

---

[13]Revelation 20:6

[14]The people of Babel, which later became known as Babylonia or Chaldea, were not trying to literally build their way to heaven. This popular myth is wrong. The Babylonians were not stupid, they were master builders from a very sophisticated culture! The tower was built for star worship. The Babylonians were the inventors of astrology. God scattered them and confused their language because of their disobedience. God told Noah and his sons to *Be fruitful and replenish the earth (Gen 9:1)*. However we find in Gen 11:1-2 that the whole of mankind had travelled to the land of Shinar and settled there and had not replenished the earth as they had been commanded. It is evident too from their comment in Gen 11:4, *...let us make us a name lest we be scattered abroad upon the face of the whole earth*, that they knew God had commanded them to split up and replenish the earth. They had deliberately defied God! It is also clear from Gen 10:8-10 that Nimrod was the first world dictator. In scattering them and confusing their language, God ensured that separate countries were established under individual government.

successful world government, and, as was the case in Genesis chapter 11 and will be the case under the Beast's rule, there is always the danger of a ruthless dictatorship.

The fourth seal – the pale horse – death (Revelation 6:7-8)

And when he had opened the fourth seal, I heard the voice of the fourth beast say, Come and see. And I looked, and behold a pale horse: and his name that sat on him was Death, and Hell followed with him. And power was given unto them over the fourth part of the earth, to kill with sword, and with hunger, and with death, and with the beasts of the earth. (Revelation 6:7-8)

The word *pale* is 'Chloros' from which we get the word chlorine. Upon this ethereal horse was seated a rider called *Death*, and *Hell* followed with him. *Death* and *Hell* were given power to kill one out of every four people. The weapons of *Death* are: sword, hunger, death, the beasts of the earth. [15]In the Old Testament God warned the Jews of these same divine judgements because of their disobedience. Now in Revelation, God sends these judgements upon the whole world. The rider *Death* does not bring meaningless destruction; this is a divine judgement upon a sinful world. [16]God warns of the four horsemen so that people may heed the warning, repent and trust in the Lord Jesus Christ and be saved from the torment of Hell.

---

[15]e.g. Leviticus 26:21-26, Ezekiel 14:21-23

[16]John 3:16-18

The fifth seal (Revelation 6:9-11)

And when he had opened the fifth seal, I saw under the altar the souls of them that were slain for the word of God, and for the testimony which they held: And they cried with a loud voice, saying, How long, O Lord, holy and true, dost thou not judge and avenge our blood on them that dwell on the earth? And white robes were given unto every one of them; and it was said unto them, that they should rest yet for a little season, until their fellowservants also and their brethren, that should be killed as they were, should be fulfilled. (Revelation 6:9-11)

In order to understand the position of the souls under the altar, it is necessary to have a basic understanding of what happens after death. In the main, two words, 'Sheol' in the Old Testament, and 'Hadës' in the New Testament are variously translated as 'the grave', 'the pit' and 'Hell' in the Authorized King James Version of the Bible. Other Bible translations insert the words 'Sheol' and 'Hadës' directly into the text with no attempt at translation. In the following passages I have inserted the original word in square brackets un-italicized. It can be considered that the Old Testament 'Sheol' is equivalent to the New Testament 'Hadës' up to the time of Christ's ascension.

Sheol

Sheol was a place of silence and suspended activity:

...in death there is no remembrance of thee: in the grave [Sheol] *who shall give thee thanks. (Psalm 6:5)*

...the grave [Sheol] *cannot praise thee, death can not celebrate thee: they that go down into the pit cannot hope for thy truth. (Isaiah 38:18)*

78

But there is prophecy of change from this state of mere survival to a better state:

I will ransom them from the power of the grave [Sheol]*; I will redeem them from death... (Hosea 13:14)*

Sheol was the abode of both the righteous dead and the unrighteous dead at this time. However we are told that the righteous will be redeemed from the power of the grave while the unrighteous will be cut off from God's presence:

...the wicked is reserved to the day of destruction... they shall be brought forth to the day of wrath (Job 21:30)

He [God] *is swift as the waters; their* [the wicked's] *portion is cursed in the earth: he beholdeth not the way of the vineyards. Drought and heat consume the snow waters: so doth the grave* [Sheol] *those which have sinned. (Job 24:18-19)*

Like sheep they [that trust in riches] *are laid in the grave* [Sheol]*; death shall feed on them; and the upright shall have dominion over them in the morning; and their beauty shall consume in the grave* [Sheol] *from their dwelling. But God will redeem my soul from the power of the grave* [Sheol]*: for he shall receive me. (Psalm 49:14-15)*

I made the nations to shake at the sound of his [the Assyrian nation's] *fall, when I cast him down to hell* [Sheol] *with them that descend into the pit: and all the trees of Eden* [i.e. the righteous] *, the choice and best of Lebanon, all that drink water, shall be comforted in the nether parts of the earth. (Ezekiel 31:16-16)*

The righteous and unrighteous both went to Sheol at death. Let us look at Christ's teaching on this subject:

79

There was a certain rich man, which was clothed in purple and fine linen, and fared sumptuously every day: And there was a certain beggar named Lazarus, which was laid at his gate, full of sores, and desiring to be fed with the crumbs which fell from the rich man's table: moreover the dogs came and licked his sores. And it came to pass, that the beggar died, and was carried by the angels into Abraham's bosom: the rich man also died, and was buried; And in hell [Hadës] *he lift up his eyes, being in torments, and seeth Abraham afar off, and Lazarus in his bosom. And he cried and said, Father Abraham, have mercy on me, and send Lazarus, that he may dip the tip of his finger in water, and cool my tongue; for I am tormented in this flame. But Abraham said, Son, remember that thou in thy lifetime receivedst thy good things, and likewise Lazarus evil things: but now he is comforted and thou art tormented. And beside all this, between us and you there is a great gulf fixed: so that they which would pass from hence to you cannot: neither can they pass to us, that would come from thence... (Luke 16:19-26)*

Luke 16:23-24 shows that the unrighteous in Hadës are conscious, have full use of their faculties, and are in torment. Christ says here that Hadës (which at this time, i.e. before Christ's ascension, was still equivalent to Sheol) was divided into two parts:

One part was Paradise – in Luke 23:43 Jesus promised the penitent thief who was crucified with Him, ...*today shalt thou be with me in paradise*, meaning the righteous part of Hadës, which is sometimes called by the Jews 'Abraham's bosom', which is why Jesus used this term in Luke 16:22.

The other part of Hadës was called 'Gehenna' and is described by Jesus in Matthew 23:33 as a place of torment, *Ye serpents, ye generation of vipers, how can ye escape the damnation of hell* [Gehenna]*?'*

All this that we've looked at so far is the past situation. The turning point from the past to the present situation was the ascension of Christ:

[17]Ephesians 4:8-10 ...*When he ascended up on high, he led captivity captive, and gave gifts unto men. (Now that he ascended, what is it but that he also descended first into the lower parts of the earth? He that descended is the same also that ascended up far above all heavens, that he might fill all things.)*

In the original quote from Psalm 68:18, the word *captive* comes from the Hebrew word 'shabah' which means 'to take away captive'. Consequently, it could be rendered thus:

When he ascended on high, he led captive a host of captives, and gave gifts to men. (Ephesians 4:8).

Ephesians 4:9, *he also descended first into the lower parts of the earth* means that when Christ died, He went to the (pre-ascension) part of Hadës that was called Paradise, or Abraham's bosom, ...*today shalt thou be with me in paradise (Luke 23:43).*

Ephesians 4:8, ... *When he ascended on high, he led captive a host of captives...* means that when Christ ascended, He led the souls of the righteous from Paradise in Hadës, to Heaven.

Now, after Christ's ascension, when the righteous die they no longer go to Paradise in Hadës, but to be with their resurrected Lord in Heaven itself. Now, after Christ's ascension, Hadës is no longer equivalent to Sheol; Hadës is equivalent to Gehenna, the place of torment for the souls of the unrighteous, – *Ye*

---

[17]Ephesians 4:8 is a quote from Psalm 68:18

serpents, ye generation of vipers, how can ye escape the damnation of hell [Gehenna]*? (Matthew 23:33).*

Paradise

Before Christ's ascension, Paradise meant the righteous part of Hadës/Sheol. [18]Now, after Christ's ascension, [19]Paradise means Heaven itself. There is another Paradise to come. This will be the heavenly city, New Jerusalem on the new earth which will be created when this current earth has been destroyed:

And I saw a new heaven and a new earth: for the first heaven and the first earth were passed away; and there was no more sea. And I John saw the holy city, new Jerusalem, coming down from God out of heaven... (Revelation 21:1-2)

In the midst of the street of it, and on either side of the river, was there the tree of life... (Revelation 22:2)

...To him that overcometh will I give to eat of the tree of life, which is in the midst of the paradise of God (Revelation 2:7).

---

[18]e.g. 2 Corinthians 12:2-4. Paul describes how he was *caught up to the third heaven (2 Cor 12:2)*; he also describes this place as *paradise (2 Cor 12:4)*. It is possible that this experience was a result of his being stoned and left for dead (Acts 14:19-20). The Bible uses the word 'heaven' in three senses:

    1) The atmosphere, or the air (e.g. Jeremiah 4:25)

    2) Outer space, sun, moon, stars, etc. (e.g. Psalm 8:3)

    3) The third heaven, which is the abode of God (e.g. 2 Cor 12:2)

[19]Until the Rapture, Heaven/Paradise is still a place of suspended activity; they are *asleep in Jesus (1 Thessalonians 4:14)*. It is at the Rapture that they are changed to be like Him and become active.

So Paradise is wherever the soul of the <u>believer</u> is, in the presence of God:

Psalm 139:8	Sheol	(Past)
2 Cor 12:4	Heaven	(Present)
Revelation 2:7; 21:1-2; 22:2	New Jerusalem	(Future)

Gehenna

Gehenna means 'Valley of Hinnom', or [20]'the valley of the sons of Hinnom'; it is a deep, narrow glen to the south of Jerusalem, where the idolatrous Jews offered their children in sacrifice to Molech. Afterward it became the common place for all the refuse of the city. Dead bodies of animals, criminals and all kinds of filth, were cast in and consumed by an everlasting fire. It inevitably became known as the place of everlasting destruction.

What is it like in Gehenna?

The rich man said *I am tormented in this flame (Luke 16:24)*

Christ spoke of the unrighteous going *...into hell* [Gehenna]*, into the fire that never shall be quenched: Where their worm dieth not...' (Mark 9:43-44)*

---

[20] e.g. 2 Chr 28:3; 33:6; Jer 7:31; 19:2-6

It could well be that the fire and torment is due to the
[21]unrighteous soul having no body: When the body dies, the soul
lives on. The soul is the part that contains the appetites, desires
and emotions. When the soul leaves the body at death, it takes
these with it. When the Christian dies and goes to Heaven, the
sinful parts of the soul are [22]burned up or taken away, because a
holy [23]God cannot have sin in His presence. But when the
unrighteous die, their soul lives on complete with all its former
appetites, desires and emotions. Those who gave themselves up
to lusts on earth will burn because they have no body with
which to fulfil those lusts! The rich man who fared sumptuously
every day (Luke 16:19) evidently had in his soul the sensation
of thirst, but he had no way of fulfilling his soul's desire
because he had no body. Here, surely, is the torment: Appetites
and desires growing more and more intense and no way of
satisfying them! Truly *...a worm* [that] *dieth not... (Mark 9:43-44).*

Perhaps I oversimplify, but here we see the justice of God in
punishing the unbelieving soul. Those who led an otherwise
'good' life not burning so severely as the 'very wicked'
unbeliever. Again, in simple terms, the punishment fits the
crime.

---

[21] 1 Corinthians chapter 15: the Christian soul is given a new body at Christ's
return

[22] 1 Corinthians 3:10-15

[23] This is why God had to abandon Jesus when He bore our sins on the cross:

Matthew 27:46 *And about the ninth hour Jesus cried with a loud voice, saying,
Eli, Eli, lama sabachthani? that is to say, My God, my God, why hast thou
forsaken me?*

2 Corinthians 5:21 *For he hath made him to be sin for us, who knew no sin; that
we might be made the righteousness of God in him.*

Back to the souls under the altar of Revelation 6:9

Bear in mind the time of this verse. The church is already translated or raptured by this time: Christians will be taken out of the world before the Beast is revealed: 2 Thess 2:7 *For the mystery of iniquity doth already work: only he who now letteth* [or hinders] *will let, until he be taken out of the way and then shall that wicked be revealed....*

The One who is restraining evil is the Holy Spirit, indwelling Christians. When He is taken out of the world at the rapture of the Church, when believers are taken up to be with Christ, evil will be unrestrained in the world *...and then shall that wicked* [the Beast] *be revealed.*

Satan will make war against those who have come to believe in Christ during the tribulation period: Revelation 12:17 *And the dragon* [Satan] *was wroth with the woman* [Israel], *and went to make war with the remnant of her seed, which keep the commandments of God, and have the testimony of Jesus Christ.* Even after the rapture of the church, God will be eager for those remaining on the earth to believe in the Lord Jesus Christ, and so, even though we are told in 2 Thess 2:11-12 that *...God shall send them strong delusion, that they should believe a lie* [the lies of the Beast]*: That they all might be damned who believed not the truth, but had pleasure in unrighteousness*, He will send the Holy Spirit back into the world after the translation of the Church, in the form of His two witnesses. Revelation 11:3 says *And I will give power unto my two witnesses, and they shall prophesy a thousand two hundred and threescore days, clothed in sackcloth.*

From what we are told in Zechariah chapter 4 and Revelation chapter 11, we suspect that these two witnesses are [24]either Moses and Elijah, or Enoch and Elijah:

Zechariah 4:11-14 *What are these two olive trees upon the right side of the [25]candlestick and upon the left side thereof? And I answered again, and said unto him, What be these two olive branches which through the two golden pipes empty the golden [26]oil out of themselves? And he answered me and said, Knowest thou not what these be? And I said, No, my lord. Then said he, These are the two anointed ones, that [27]stand by the Lord of the whole earth.*

Revelation 11:3-4 *And I will give power unto my two witnesses, and they shall prophesy a thousand two hundred and threescore days, clothed in sackcloth. These are the two olive trees, and the two candlesticks standing before the God of the earth.*

Revelation 11:6 *These have power to [28]shut heaven, that it rain not in the days of their prophecy: and have power over [29]waters to turn them to blood, and to smite the earth with all plagues, as often as they will.*

---

[24] See chapter 11

[25] The Church (Revelation 1:20)

[26] The two witnesses (anointed one) are filled with the Holy Spirit, symbolised by the oil.

[27] Moses and Elijah were standing by the Lord at His transfiguration (Matthew 17:1-4)

[28] 1 Kings 17:1

[29] Exodus 7:19-21

[30]Those who come to believe in the Lord Jesus Christ during the tribulation period will be killed for their faith. These are the ones whose souls are under the altar in Revelation 6:9. These tribulation period believers who have been killed for their faith are told to *rest yet for a little season, until their fellowservants also and their brethren, that should be killed as they were, should be fulfilled. (Revelation 6:11)*. Evidently the number of those who would be killed for their faith during the tribulation period was not yet complete. In Revelation 7:9-17 their number is complete.

[31]The sixth seal (Revelation 6:12-17)

And I beheld when he had opened the sixth seal, and, lo, there was a great earthquake; and the sun became black as sackcloth of hair, and the moon became as blood; And the stars of heaven fell unto the earth, even as a fig tree casteth her untimely figs, when she is shaken of a mighty wind. And the heaven departed as a scroll when it is rolled together; and every mountain and island were moved out of their places. And the kings of the earth, and the great men, and the rich men, and the chief captains, and the mighty men, and every bondman, and every free man, [32]hid themselves in the dens and in the rocks of the mountains; And said to the mountains and rocks, Fall on us, and hide us from the face of him that sitteth on the throne, and from the wrath of the

---

[30] Revelation 12:17, 13:15

[31] This is the start of *that determined* [which] *shall be poured upon the desolate* (desolator) *(Dan 9:27)*. Revelation chapters 8 and 16 contain the full account of *that determined*.

[32] Compare Isaiah 2:19

Lamb: For the great day of his wrath is come; and who shall be able to stand? (Revelation 6:12-17)

Matthew 24:6-8 says *And ye shall hear of wars and rumours of wars: see that ye be not troubled: for all these things must come to pass, but the end is not yet. For nation shall rise against nation, and kingdom against kingdom: and there shall be famines, and pestilences, and earthquakes, in divers places. All these are the beginning of sorrows.*

These are the signs of the end of the age (Mt 24:3). The great earthquake in Revelation 6:12 is more than just a sign; it appears to be a precursor to the opening of the seventh seal which is composed of seven trumpets, and signifies the start of the great tribulation: the final 3½ years of the Beast's rule. There are signs here however, that the day of the Lord is approaching: Compare Joel 2:31 *The sun shall be turned into darkness, and the moon into blood, before the great and terrible day of the LORD come.*

It is unclear whether this *great earthquake* is worldwide or local to the ten kingdoms over which the Beast has dominion (represented by the ten horns of the Beast (Revelation 13:1). We can only guess the source of this *great earthquake*. It could be natural, man-made, or a direct act of God. One possible man-made source comes from passive nuclear weapons which are reputedly sited on the earth's crust where tectonic plates meet and in high mountain ranges. [33]These passive weapons are in

---

[33]Every weapons system depends on geo-physical parameters, e.g. gravity, motion and the speed of light, for guidance; satellite based weapons systems would also depend on astro-physical constants. If the world were to be shaken by these passive nuclear weapons, the geo-physical and astro-physical constants would be suspended. The parameters required for weapons navigation would be

place to shake the world if a nuclear strike is expected. Whatever the cause however, we can be sure that it is in God's control and the time of it will be according to His plan.

---

unavailable. Moreover an electromagnetic pulse would disable most electronic devices. Weapons guidance systems would be useless.

7

Revelation chapter 7:
144000 Jews and the Gentile multitude

And after these things I saw four angels standing on the four corners of the earth, holding the four winds of the earth, that the wind should not blow on the earth, nor on the sea, nor on any tree. And I saw another angel ascending from the east, having the seal of the living God: and he cried with a loud voice to the four angels, to whom it was given to hurt the earth and the sea, Saying, Hurt not the earth, neither the sea, nor the trees, till we have sealed the servants of our God in their foreheads. (Revelation 7:1-3)

Here we have a period of calm before the opening of the seventh seal of God's judgement upon the earth in Revelation chapter 8. Four angels are depicted as *standing on the four corners of the earth, holding the four winds of the earth, that the wind should not blow on the earth, nor on the sea, nor on any tree (Revelation 7:1)*. These actually have the task *to hurt the earth and the sea (Revelation 7:2)* but are commanded to hold back *till we have sealed the servants of our God in their foreheads (Revelation 7:3)*. The [1]seal that these servants of God are to receive is that of the Holy Spirit.

---

[1]Ephesians 1:13-14. See also the narrative on Revelation 5:1

And I heard the number of them which were sealed: and there were sealed an hundred and forty and four thousand of all the tribes of the children of Israel. (Revelation 7:4)

The probable origin of the 144000 Jews is outlined below together with an overall picture of the events leading up to their conversion:

- There is coming a day when [2]Christ will take His church out of the world.

- With the church removed, [3]evil is unrestrained in the world. [4]The Beast will be revealed, and, for a time he will seem to have solutions to the world's problems. [5]He will even allow the Jews to re-commence the kind of sacrificial worship that we read of in the Old Testament.

- As time goes on however, his reign will become more cruel and dictatorial.

- After 3½ years he will seat himself in the temple at Jerusalem, declare himself to be God, and demand [6]worship.

- At this point the Jews will realise that the Lord Jesus Christ, whom they had rejected for so long, is indeed

---

[2] 1 Thess 4:16-17; 1 Cor 15:51-52; 2 Thess 2:1-12

[3] 2 Thess 2:7

[4] 2 Thess 2:8

[5] Dan 9:27

[6] 2 Thess 2:3-4

their promised Messiah, and 144,000 of them will now turn to Him in faith.

Why is the tribe of Dan not counted among the 144000?

In Numbers chapter 1, the twelve tribes of Israel are listed. If we compare this Old Testament listing against the tribes listed in Revelation chapter 7:5-8, we find that there is one important difference:

O.T. Tribes (Num ch 1)	N.T. Tribes (Revelation ch 7)
Reuben	Yes
Simeon	Yes
Judah	Yes
Issachar	Yes
Zebulun	Yes
Joseph (Ephraim)	Yes
Manasseh	Yes
Benjamin	Yes
Dan	No, Levi included instead
Asher	Yes
Naphtali	Yes
Gad	Yes

Originally, in the Old Testament, even though they were
sometimes described as a tribe, e.g. *Bring near the tribe of
Levi... (Numbers 3:6)*, Levi was not properly counted as a tribe.
Instead they were set apart for priestly duties. However when
we come to the list of tribes in Revelation chapter 7, Levi is
counted as a tribe but Dan is not. Why? Let us look at the tribe
of Dan:

The idolatry of Dan

Judges 17:5-11 *And the man Micah had an house of gods, and
made an ephod, and teraphim... And there was a young man
out of Bethlehemjudah of the family of Judah, who was a
Levite, and he sojourned there. And the man departed out of
the city from Bethlehemjudah to sojourn where he could find a
place: and he came to mount Ephraim to the house of Micah,
as he journeyed. And Micah said unto him, Whence comest
thou? And he said unto him, I am a Levite of Bethlehemjudah,
and I go to sojourn where I may find a place. And Micah said
unto him, Dwell with me, and be unto me a father and a
priest... So the Levite went in. And the Levite was content to
dwell with the man...*

Judges 18:1-3 *...in those days the tribe of the Danites sought
them an inheritance to dwell in; for unto that day all their
inheritance had not fallen unto them among the tribes of Israel.
And the children of Dan sent of their family five men from their
coasts, men of valour, from Zorah, and from Eshtaol, to spy out
the land, and to search it; and they said unto them, Go, search
the land: who when they came to mount Ephraim, to the house
of Micah, they lodged there. When they were by the house of
Micah, they knew the voice of the young man the Levite: and
they turned in thither...*

Judges 18:11-18 *And there went from thence of the family of the
Danites, out of Zorah and out of Eshtaol, six hundred men*

appointed with weapons of war... And they... came unto the house of Micah. Then answered the five men that went to spy out the country of Laish, and said unto their brethren, Do ye know that there is in these houses an ephod, and teraphim, and a graven image, and a molten image? now therefore consider what ye have to do. And they turned thitherward, and came to the house of the young man the Levite, even unto the house of Micah, and saluted him. And the six hundred men appointed with their weapons of war, which were of the children of Dan, stood by the entering of the gate. And the five men that went to spy out the land went up, and came in thither, and took the graven image, and the ephod, and the teraphim, and the molten image: and the priest stood in the entering of the gate with the six hundred men that were appointed with weapons of war. And these went into Micah's house, and fetched the carved image, the ephod, and the teraphim, and the molten image...

Judges 18:27-31 *And they took the things which Micah had made, and the priest which he had, and came unto Laish, unto a people that were at quiet and secure: and they smote them with the edge of the sword, and burnt the city with fire. ...And they built a city, and dwelt therein. And they called the name of the city Dan, after the name of Dan their father, who was born unto Israel: howbeit the name of the city was Laish at the first. And the children of Dan set up the graven image: and Jonathan, the son of Gershom, the son of Manasseh, he and his sons were priests to the tribe of Dan until the day of the captivity of the land. And they set them up Micah's graven image, which he made, all the time that the house of God was in Shiloh.*

King Jeroboam caused Israel to worship idols in the town of Dan

1 Kings 12:28-30 *...the king took counsel, and made two calves of gold, and said unto them, It is too much for you to go up to Jerusalem: behold thy gods, O Israel, which brought thee up*

out of the land of Egypt. And he set the one in Bethel, and the other put he in Dan. And this thing became a sin: for the people went to worship before the one, even unto Dan.

Jacob's prophecy concerning Dan

Genesis 49:1 *And Jacob called unto his sons, and said, Gather yourselves together, that I may tell you that which shall befall you in the last days.*

Genesis 49:17 *Dan shall be a serpent by the way, an adder in the path, that biteth the horse heels, so that his rider shall fall backward.*

This prophecy indicates Dan's treachery in the last days.

The tribe of Dan are probably those who Jesus referred to who will be deceived, when He said *For there shall arise false Christs, and false prophets, and shall shew great signs and wonders; insomuch that, if it were possible, they shall deceive the very elect. (Matthew 24:24)*

The reign of the Beast during the tribulation period is just such a time when false messiahs will perform *great signs and wonders*:

Revelation 13:11-15 *And I beheld another beast coming up out of the earth; and he had two horns like a lamb, and he spake as a dragon. And he exerciseth all the power of the first beast before him, and causeth the earth and them which dwell therein to worship the first beast, whose deadly wound was healed. And he doeth great wonders, so that he maketh fire come down from heaven on the earth in the sight of men, And deceiveth them that dwell on the earth by the means of those miracles which he had power to do in the sight of the beast; saying to them that dwell on the earth, that they should make an image to the beast, which*

*had the wound by a sword, and did live. And he had power to
give life unto the image of the beast, that the image of the beast
should both speak, and cause that as many as would not
worship the image of the beast should be killed.*

To sum up

- The tribe of Dan will not be represented among the
  144000 Jews redeemed during the tribulation period.

- They have a strong tendency toward idol worship.

- They are probably those referred to in Matthew 24:24
  who will be deceived.

- Being deceived they will worship the Beast when they
  see the signs, wonders, and miracles that will accompany
  his reign.

- The Danites will not be counted among God's people
  even though outside observers may have thought them to
  be blessed by God.

The Beast will almost certainly be, or will be seen to be, a Jew;
otherwise it is unlikely that the Jewish nation would accept him
as their leader and allow him to *confirm the covenant with many
(Daniel 9:27)*. It also seems likely that he will have a strong
following from the tribe of Dan. It is clear that the tribe of Dan
is counted among those to whom *God shall send them strong
delusion, that they should believe a lie: That they all might be
damned who believed not the truth, but had pleasure in
unrighteousness. (2 Thess 2:11-12).*

Dan is probably omitted because of their tendency toward idol
worship. In 1 Kings 12:28-30 Dan induced the other tribes to
sin in this way too. God will not allow this; it seems that Dan is

omitted from the 144,000 to stop them leading tribulation period Jews astray.

Are there any modern Danites?

[7]There are many, non-Jewish, 'Danites'. Obvious examples are the [8]Roman Catholic Church and the Church of England. These may use familiar forms of worship (just as the Danites used a Levite). They expect God's blessing even though they practise idolatry (e.g. Icon worship, Mary worship) and even though God's word has been altered, ignored or sometimes reversed through the [9]notion that some biblical doctrines are out of touch with the modern world.

The familiar forms of worship are used and the unbeliever sees nothing amiss. Those who have 'modernised' the Gospel (e.g. the Church of England with their women priests) may even look inviting to the world, <u>but there is error</u>.

---

[7]Compare what God says in Exodus 20:3-5, *Thou shalt have no other gods before me. Thou shalt not make unto thee any graven image, or any likeness of any thing that is in heaven above, or that is in the earth beneath, or that is in the water under the earth: Thou shalt not bow down thyself to them, nor serve them: for I the LORD thy God am a jealous God, visiting the iniquity of the fathers upon the children unto the third and fourth generation of them that hate me.*

[8]See also chapter 17. These institutions are not devoid of genuine Christians but are guilty of gross doctrinal error.

[9]The <u>fact</u> of the matter is that the world is out of touch with biblical doctrine, not the other way round!

A great multitude

[10]After this I beheld, and, lo, a great multitude, which no man could number, of all nations, and kindreds, and people, and tongues, stood before the throne, and before the Lamb, clothed with white robes, and [11]palms in their hands... These are they which came out of great tribulation, and have washed their robes, and made them white in the blood of the Lamb. (Revelation 7:9, 14)

The point at which the Beast *sitteth in the temple of God, shewing himself that he is God (2 Thess 2:4)* marks the start of the Great Tribulation, which will last for [12]3½ years. That life will be very difficult for those who come to believe during the Beast's reign is, to say the least, an understatement. Below are a few verses which show some of the difficulties which they will face:

Revelation 13:7-8 *And it was given unto him* [the Beast] *to make war with the saints, and to overcome them: and power was given him over all kindreds, and tongues, and nations. And all that dwell upon the earth shall worship him, whose names are not written in the book of life of the Lamb slain from the foundation of the world.*

Revelation 13:11-17 *And I beheld another beast coming up out of the earth; and he had two horns like a lamb, and he spake as a dragon. And he exerciseth all the power of the first beast*

---

[10] See also chapter 12: 'Those who come to Christ during the tribulation period are persecuted', and chapter 13.

[11] These palms are a symbol of victory and peace.

[12] Dan 9:27; Revelation 13:5

before him, and causeth the earth and them which dwell therein to worship the first beast, whose deadly wound was healed. And he doeth great wonders, so that he maketh fire come down from heaven on the earth in the sight of men, and deceiveth them that dwell on the earth by the means of those miracles which he had power to do in the sight of the beast; saying to them that dwell on the earth, that they should make an image to the beast, which had the wound by a sword, and did live. And he had power to give life unto the image of the beast, that the image of the beast should both speak, and cause that as many as would not worship the image of the beast should be killed. And he causeth all, both small and great, rich and poor, free and bond, to receive a mark in their right hand, or in their foreheads: And that no man might buy or sell, save he that had the mark, or the name of the beast, or the number of his name.

These believers will be martyred. Unable to worship the Beast, as he demands of them, they will die for their faith. If they go undetected, they will be unable to make a living; they will not be allowed to buy or sell without first receiving the mark of the Beast, whatever form that may take. So, it will be hard for them to exist at all, and, when they are caught they will have to decide: to worship the Beast, or to defy the Beast and suffer what will probably involve public humiliation before being killed for their faith.

It is interesting to note that even after Christ has removed His church from the world at the Rapture, those who will come to believe during the tribulation period are still saved through the blood of Christ – there is no other way to salvation:

Revelation 7:14 ...*These are they which came out of great tribulation, and have washed their robes, and made them white* ***in the blood of the Lamb***.

The last few verses of this chapter give us a glimpse of life during Christ's 1000 year reign on earth after the Beast and the False Prophet have been [13]*cast alive into a lake of fire burning with brimstone* and [14]Satan has been bound for a thousand years:

Revelation 7:15-17 *Therefore are they before the throne of God, and serve him day and night in his temple: and he that sitteth on the throne shall dwell among them. They shall hunger no more, neither thirst any more; neither shall the sun light on them, nor any heat. For the Lamb which is in the midst of the throne shall feed them, and shall lead them unto living fountains of waters: and God shall wipe away all tears from their eyes.*

---

[13]Revelation 19:20

[14]Revelation 20:2-3

8

Revelation chapter 8:
The opening of the seventh seal –
trumpets one to four

The seven trumpet events will take place during the time known as the Great Tribulation: that time when the world's ruler, the Beast of Revelation chapter 13, will declare himself to be God and will sit in the temple at Jerusalem and demand worship. Let us take a moment to set the scene and to see what the world situation will be, before we look into the contents of this chapter:

- [1]The church will have been translated 3½ years before the events of this chapter.

- [2]Initially the Beast will have allowed the Jews to reinstate their old style of sacrificial worship.

- [3]After 3½ years however, he will break this covenant. [4]He will declare himself to be God and sit in the temple at Jerusalem [5]demanding worship. [6]He will receive it.

---

[1]1 Cor 15:50-54, 1 Thess 4:13-17, 2 Thess 2:7

[2]Daniel 9:27

[3]Daniel 9:27

[4]2 Thess 2:4

[5]Revelation 13:12

Revelation chapter 8:
The opening of the seventh seal –
trumpets one to four

[7]The penalty for not bowing down to the Beast will be death.

There are diversities of opinion about the meaning and nature of events that occur during the Great Tribulation. Some scholars will allude to spiritual meanings for the calamities that are described. However, I believe that these events are quite literal, though symbolisms are used, as is the case generally in the book of Revelation. The events are obviously open to various interpretations. The explanations that I have placed on them are my own thoughts and I cannot say whether they are right or wrong. The simple truth is that nobody can accurately define these events or even say whether these judgements of God are natural or supernatural phenomena. Some of these ideas may seem fantastic but I will set them forth and the reader will judge!

And when he had opened the seventh seal, there was silence in heaven about the space of half an hour. (Revelation 8:1)

The opening of the seventh seal completes the opening of the seven sealed book which started in Revelation 5:1. The opening of this seal will allow the contents of the trumpets (Revelation ch 8) and vials (Revelation ch 16) to be released upon the earth. Revelation chapters 8 and 16 both describe calamitous events that will occur during this time in the world's history. The half an hour of silence is a lull after the great earthquake (sixth seal), and is the prelude to the cataclysmic events that will happen following the opening of the seventh seal.

---

[6]Revelation 13:12

[7]Revelation 13:15

Revelation chapter 8:
The opening of the seventh seal –
trumpets one to four

And I saw the seven angels which stood before God; and to them were given seven trumpets. And another angel came and stood at the altar, having a golden censer; and there was given unto him much incense, that he should offer it with the prayers of all saints upon the golden altar which was before the throne. And the smoke of the incense, which came with the prayers of the saints, ascended up before God out of the angel's hand. And the angel took the censer, and filled it with fire of the altar, and cast it into the earth: and there were voices, and thunderings, and lightnings, and an earthquake. And the seven angels which had the seven trumpets prepared themselves to sound. (Revelation 8:2-6)

Incense has always been connected with the prayers of God's people, as symbolising that which makes prayer acceptable to God: the intercession of Christ. The symbolism is used here to illustrate that the *voices, and thunderings, and lightnings, and an earthquake (Revelation 8:5)* are in answer to *the prayers of the saints (Revelation 8:4)*. This event is the righteous anger of God: *fire from the altar*, poured out upon an evil world in answer to the prayers of His people. It is also the signal for the start of the seven trumpet judgements:

The first trumpet (Revelation 8:7)

The first angel sounded, and there followed hail and fire mingled with blood, and they were cast upon the earth: and the third part of trees was burnt up, and all green grass was burnt up. (Revelation 8:7)

The first angel sounded his trumpet *and there followed* [8]*hail and fire mingled with blood.* [9]An electrical storm of an intensity that

---

[8]Compare Revelation 16:21

Revelation chapter 8:
The opening of the seventh seal –
trumpets one to four

the world has never seen before. Such will be its power that the Bible says *the third part of trees was burnt up, and all green grass was burnt up*. This will not be a localised storm but will be worldwide and utterly catastrophic.

The second trumpet (Revelation 8:8-9)

And the second angel sounded, and as it were a great mountain burning with fire was cast into the sea: and the third part of the sea became blood; And the third part of the creatures which were in the sea, and had life, died; and the third part of the ships were destroyed. (Revelation 8:8-9)

A *great mountain burning with fire* is cast into the sea. The most likely explanation that I can think of is that this is a giant meteorite, which, as it enters the earth's atmosphere, gets hot, its surface aflame. We are told that it is like *a great mountain*, so it could well be hundreds of miles in diameter! Perhaps the cataclysmic electrical storm of verse 7 (the first trumpet) is a result of the approach of this giant meteorite. The approach of a meteorite of this size would spark off all manner of freak conditions on the earth. This gigantic meteorite is so large that when it falls into the sea *the third part of the sea became blood; And the third part of the creatures which were in the sea, and had life, died; and the third part of the ships were destroyed*. Usually a large meteorite is accompanied by other, smaller meteorites and meteors. If the main meteorite is several hundreds of miles in diameter, then those accompanying it could well be of substantial proportions also. Given the conditions that would follow such a meteorite falling into the

---

[9] See also 'The second trumpet (Revelation 8:8-9)'

Revelation chapter 8:
The opening of the seventh seal –
trumpets one to four

sea (tidal waves etc.) the consequences described are quite in accordance with such an event.

The third trumpet (Revelation 8:10-11)

And the third angel sounded, and there fell a great star from heaven, burning as it were a lamp, and it fell upon the third part of the rivers, and upon the fountains of waters; And the name of the star is called Wormwood: and the third part of the waters became wormwood; and many men died of the waters, because they were made bitter. (Revelation 8:10-11)

The literal translation of the word *wormwood* is 'wormwood' or 'undrinkable'. The *great star from heaven, burning as it were a lamp* could be a spirit, in a similar sense to that used in Revelation 4:5, *there were seven lamps of fire burning before the throne, which are the seven Spirits of God*, but since spirits usually travel unseen in the heavenly realm, it is likely that a more literal translation is called for and that this *great star from heaven, burning as it were a lamp* is another meteorite. It is suspected by some that meteorites and more particularly space dust, which travels slowly through the atmosphere and therefore doesn't burn up, contain bacteria. As the bacteria-infected space dust falls to the earth, the bacteria is spread out over a large area and is said to be the reason why some [10]disease affects people over a large area simultaneously (if it was transmitted from person to person it should spread slowly). It could be that such a mechanism will infect a third of the earth's fresh water, make it undrinkable and cause many deaths from drinking the infected water. The bacteria could be spread worldwide by infected

---

[10] It is also said that this is why new diseases and viruses are being caught and discovered all the time: because they are literally new to this earth.

Revelation chapter 8:
The opening of the seventh seal –
trumpets one to four

debris accompanying this large meteorite, or perhaps the meteorite might break up upon impact with the earth's surface and release bacteria from within.

The fourth trumpet (Revelation 8:12-13)

And the fourth angel sounded, and the third part of the sun was smitten, and the third part of the moon, and the third part of the stars; so as the third part of them was darkened, and the day shone not for a third part of it, and the night likewise. (Revelation 8:12)

And the fourth angel poured out his vial upon the sun; and power was given unto him to scorch men with fire. And men were scorched with great heat... (Revelation 16:8-9)

Behold, the day of the LORD cometh, cruel both with wrath and fierce anger... For the stars of heaven and the constellations thereof shall not give their light: the sun shall be darkened in his going forth, and the moon shall not cause her light to shine. Therefore I will shake the heavens, and the earth shall remove out of her place, in the wrath of the LORD of hosts, and in the day of his fierce anger. (Isaiah 13:9,10,13)

It seems that after the fourth angel has sounded his trumpet the earth will no longer have a 24 hour day but a 16 hour day (Revelation 8:12). We are told that it is also the fourth angel who *poured out his vial upon the sun; and power was given unto him to scorch men with fire (Revelation 16:8)*. Since both of these events are the work of the fourth angel, it is likely that they both happen at the same time. We have seen in Revelation chapter 8 that there is going to be great calamity upon the earth. I have put forward the idea that the main catastrophe could be the fall of a giant meteorite, perhaps hundreds of miles in

Revelation chapter 8:
The opening of the seventh seal –
trumpets one to four

diameter. This would totally change the earth as we know it.
Weather patterns would be upset and there would be mass
death and destruction. It also seems feasible that a collision
with such a large [11]meteorite would knock the earth into a new
orbit slightly closer to the sun (Revelation 16:8-9). This could
explain how men become *scorched with great heat
(Revelation 16:9)*. Such an occurrence could also increase the
speed that the earth spins on its axis, shortening the day to
16 hours. This would fulfil Isaiah's prophecy: *Therefore I will
shake the heavens, and the earth shall remove out of her
place, in the wrath of the LORD of hosts, and in the day of his
fierce anger. (Isaiah 13:13).*

*And I beheld, and heard an angel flying through the midst of
heaven, saying with a loud voice, Woe, woe, woe, to the inhabiters
of the earth by reason of the other voices of the trumpet of the
three angels, which are yet to sound! (Revelation 8:13)*

Three calamities ('woes') are announced which are terrible
judgements falling not on the earth but directly upon men.
These three woes complete the final three trumpet judgements.

---

[11]It is also quite possible that this meteorite might be a particle from an even
larger object that will pass close to the earth, exerting extra gravitational force to
change the earth's orbit.

9

Revelation chapter 9: Trumpets five and six – woes one and two

The fifth trumpet: the first woe (Revelation 9:1-12)

And the fifth angel sounded, and I saw a star fall from heaven unto the earth: and to him was given the key of the bottomless pit. (Revelation 9:1)

At the trumpet of the fifth angel, a star is seen to fall from heaven and is given the key (i.e. authority) of the bottomless pit. The [1]star is evidently an angel. Whether he is an angel of God or of Satan is not entirely clear: In Revelation 9:11, *the angel of the bottomless pit* is known by the Hebrew name *Abaddon*, which in Greek is *Apollyon*. The interpretation of this name is 'Destruction' or 'Destroyer'. Clearly, *the angel of the bottomless pit* of Revelation 9:11 is either Satan or one of his angels. Yet, in Revelation 20:1-3: *And I saw an angel come down from heaven, having the key of the bottomless pit and a great chain in his hand. And he laid hold on the dragon, that old serpent, which is the Devil, and Satan, and bound him a thousand years, And cast him into the bottomless pit...*; this angel, who has the key of the bottomless pit, will bind Satan and cast him into the bottomless pit. Therefore he must be either

---

[1]Stars are sometimes symbolic of angels, e.g. Revelation 12:4

Revelation chapter 9:
Trumpets five and six –
woes one and two

an angel of God or, more likely, is the [2]Lord Jesus Christ.
Similarly, the angel of Revelation 9:1 must be either an angel of
God or the Lord Jesus Christ because it seems unlikely that God
would allow Satan or one of his followers to have custody of
the key to the bottomless pit, which is the prison for [3]demons.

*And he opened the bottomless pit; and there arose a smoke out
of the pit, as the smoke of a great furnace; and the sun and the
air were darkened by reason of the smoke of the pit. And there
came out of the smoke locusts upon the earth: and unto them
was given power, as the scorpions of the earth have power.
(Revelation 9:2-3)*

That these *locusts* are actually demons is apparent because they
will be released from the bottomless pit, the prison of demons.
The term *locusts* is used to describe them because of their
numbers: there will be so many of them that they will be like a
swarm of locusts; the smoke that *arose...out of the pit, as the
smoke of a great furnace (Revelation 9:2)* darkening the sun and
the air is another allusion to their number. Swarms of locusts
are often so large that they darken the sky and weaken the light

---

[2]I say this because of Jude 9, where even the archangel (highest rank of angel)
Michael is reluctant to directly confront Satan, preferring to leave this task to the
Lord. It therefore follows that the only one able to bind Satan and cast him into
the bottomless pit would be the Lord Jesus Christ Himself.

[3]Luke 8:30-31 *And Jesus asked him, saying, What is thy name? And he said,
Legion: because many devils were entered into him. And they besought him that
he would not command them to go out into the deep.* The word 'deep' used in the
Authorized Version, is the same Greek word 'Abussos' that is translated
bottomless pit in various parts of the book of Revelation.

There are two classes of demons: Those that are free and a worse kind that are
imprisoned in the bottomless pit, or Abyss. This latter kind will be released as
part of God's Great Tribulation judgement upon the world.

Revelation chapter 9:
Trumpets five and six –
woes one and two

from the sun. Another similarity will be their destructive nature, emphasised by the name of their king: *And they had a king over them, which is the angel of the bottomless pit, whose name in the Hebrew tongue is Abaddon, but in the Greek tongue hath his name Apollyon (Revelation 9:11)*. The interpretation of this name is 'destruction' or 'destroyer'. The sound of their approach will also be like that of locusts: *the sound of their wings was as the sound of chariots of many horses running to battle (Revelation 9:9)*.

And there came out of the smoke locusts upon the earth: and unto them was given power, as the scorpions of the earth have power. And it was commanded them that they should not hurt the grass of the earth, neither any green thing, neither any tree; but only those men which have not the seal of God in their foreheads. (Revelation 9:3-4)

Unlike real locusts, these demons are not allowed to harm any foliage. Their only target will be *men which have not the seal of God in their foreheads.* [4]There will be those who come to believe in the Lord Jesus Christ during the tribulation period; these will be protected from attack.

And to them it was given that they should not kill them, but that they should be tormented five months: and their torment was as the torment of a scorpion, when he striketh a man. And in those days shall men seek death, and shall not find it; and shall desire to die, and death shall flee from them. (Revelation 9:5-6)

These locust demons will have power *as the scorpions of the earth have power (Revelation 9:3)*. The poisonous sting of a

---

[4]See chapter 7: 'A great multitude'.

Revelation chapter 9:
Trumpets five and six –
woes one and two

scorpion causes much suffering and sometimes alarming symptoms but is not usually fatal to humans. Likewise, the attack of these demons upon men will not be fatal but the torment will be like the sting of scorpions but will last far longer. Five months is the allotted time for the torment to last! So agonising will be the pain that men will want to die. In desperation they will even try to take their own lives but *death shall flee from them*; [5]they will not be allowed to escape this judgement!

What do these locust demons look like?

And the shapes of the locusts were like unto horses prepared unto battle; and on their heads were as it were crowns like gold, and their faces were as the faces of men. And they had hair as the hair of women, and their teeth were as the teeth of lions. And they had breastplates, as it were breastplates of iron; and the sound of their wings was as the sound of chariots of many horses running to battle. And they had tails like unto scorpions, and there were stings in their tails: and their power was to hurt men five months. (Revelation 9:7-10)

- They were like *horses prepared unto battle* (vs 7)

- *on their heads were, as it were, crowns like gold* (vs 7)

- *their faces were like the faces of men* (vs 7)

- *they had hair like the hair of women* (vs 8)

- *their teeth were like the teeth of lions* (vs 8)

---

[5]This is a foretaste of Hell: See chapter 6: 'The fifth seal (Revelation 6:9-11)'.

Revelation chapter 9:
Trumpets five and six –
woes one and two

- *they had breastplates, as it were breastplates of iron* (vs 9)

- *the sound of their wings was like the sound of chariots of many horses running to battle* (vs 9)

- *they had tails like scorpions, and there were stings in their tails* (vs 10)

Are these locust demons literal or symbolic?

In time past, no doubt due to its fantastic nature, people have tried to symbolise this portion of God's word as meaning an attack of Satan upon the less faithful of Christ's church. Taken in the context of the book of Revelation as a whole, this cannot be so. Though there are symbolisms used (e.g. the star, the key, the locusts, etc.), I see no alternative but to take the judgement to be literal.

Revelation chapter 9:
Trumpets five and six –
woes one and two

*One woe is past; and, behold, there come two woes more
hereafter. (Revelation 9:12)*

The sixth trumpet: the second woe (Revelation 9:13-14)

*And the sixth angel sounded, and I heard a voice from the four
horns of the golden altar which is before God, Saying to the sixth
angel which had the trumpet, Loose the four angels which are
bound in the great river Euphrates. (Revelation 9:13-14)*

[6]The number Four is commonly accepted as the number of
universality. It is generally used when man, the world, or the
whole of creation is considered. Horns denote authority.
Therefore the single voice that is heard is that of the one who
has universal authority; it is the voice of God Himself, who
commands the four angels to be loosed. The fact that these four
angels are bound, indicates that these are Satan's angels.

*And the four angels were loosed, which were prepared for an
hour, and a day, and a month, and a year, for to slay the third
part of men. And the number of the army of the horsemen were
two hundred thousand thousand: and I heard the number of
them. And thus I saw the horses in the vision, and them that sat
on them, having breastplates of fire, and of jacinth, and
brimstone: and the heads of the horses were as the heads of lions;
and out of their mouths issued fire and smoke and brimstone. By
these three was the third part of men killed, by the fire, and by the
smoke, and by the brimstone, which issued out of their mouths.*

---

[6]e.g. Four universal monarchies (Dan ch 2 and ch 7); *the four winds of the
heaven* (Dan 7:2); The heavenly city New Jerusalem *lieth foursquare*
(Revelation 21:16); four rivers to water the garden of Eden (Gen 2:10). There are
numerous other examples.

Revelation chapter 9:
Trumpets five and six –
woes one and two

For their power is in their mouth, and in their tails: for their tails were like unto serpents, and had heads, and with them they do hurt. (Revelation 9:15-19)

These four angels *were prepared for an hour, and a day, and a month, and a year, to slay the third part of men (Revelation 9:15)*. Just as God will use the Satanic locusts to torment men for five months (Revelation 9:1-11), here He will use four of Satan's angels, together with their army of 200 million horsemen, to kill one third of the population of the earth at this time in the earth's history.

Try as I might to find some logical, rational symbolism for the description of these terrible horses and their riders, I find myself forced back to literalism. This is the time of the end: the Great Tribulation period! We should not expect the earth to be the same as before. Christ's church has been taken away! There is no restraint upon evil! I have tried to make sense of this all ways, but I have come to realise that the only way to make sense of it is to take it literally! I believe that these four Satanic angels will lead a Satanic host of 200 million demons who will *slay the third part of men* at this time.

And the rest of the men which were not killed by these plagues yet repented not of the works of their hands, that they should not worship devils, and idols of gold, and silver, and brass, and stone, and of wood: which neither can see, nor hear, nor walk: Neither repented they of their murders, nor of their sorceries, nor of their fornication, nor of their thefts. (Revelation 9:20-21)

It is a sad reflection upon mankind that he is so stubborn! And yet at this time in the earth's history, when the Holy Spirit has been removed, and when ...*God shall send* [men] *strong delusion, that they should believe a lie (2 Thessalonians 2:11)*, the odds are stacked against them. To them the lies of the Beast

Revelation chapter 9:
Trumpets five and six –
woes one and two

will seem so convincing; he will have an answer for these calamities that will befall the earth and that answer will satisfy his subjects. For the two-thirds who survive, life will continue unchanged.

10

Revelation chapter 10:
The little book

And I saw another mighty angel come down from heaven, clothed with a cloud: and a rainbow was upon his head, and his face was as it were the sun, and his feet as pillars of fire: And he had in his hand a little book open: and he set his right foot upon the sea, and his left foot on the earth, And cried with a loud voice, as when a lion roareth (Revelation 10:1-3a)

The *mighty angel... clothed with a cloud* is the Lord Jesus Christ. It is the fulfilment of the prophecy given to the disciples in Acts 1:9-11: *And when he had spoken these things, while they beheld, he was taken up; and a cloud received him out of their sight. And while they looked stedfastly toward heaven as he went up, behold, two men stood by them in white apparel; Which also said, Ye men of Galilee, why stand ye gazing up into heaven? this same Jesus, which is taken up from you into heaven, shall so come in like manner as ye have seen him go into heaven.* Another indication that this is the Lord is the [1]*rainbow... upon his head*; this is God's sign that He will never again destroy the earth by a flood. If further proof is needed, the description of this mighty angel matches that of the Lord Jesus Christ in Revelation 1:13-16: *And in the midst of the seven candlesticks one like unto the Son of man... And his feet* [were] *like unto fine brass, as if they burned in a furnace... and his*

---

[1]Genesis 8:20-22, Genesis 9:11-17, Revelation 4:3

countenance was as the sun shineth in his strength. The Lord then claims the earth as His own as He sets *his right foot upon the sea, and his left foot on the earth.* [2]The *lion* is symbolic of Christ's majesty. He is the Lord of lords and the King of kings (Revelation 17:14).

and when he had cried, seven thunders uttered their voices. And when the seven thunders had uttered their voices, I was about to write: and I heard a voice from heaven saying unto me, Seal up those things which the seven thunders uttered, and write them not. (Revelation 10:3b-4)

The *seven* [3]*thunders*, uttered by God the Father in response to the claim of His Son, shows Christ's full authority over the earth. John was about to write that which the seven thunders had uttered but was commanded not to. Obviously it is not for us to know and is proof (if it is needed!) that we cannot fully understand this book.

---

[2]See also Revelation 4:6-7

[3]Thunder, in the Bible is almost always attributed to God. There are numerous examples: e.g. John 12:28-29.

And the angel which I saw stand upon the sea and upon the earth lifted up his hand to heaven, And sware by him that liveth for ever and ever, who created heaven, and the things that therein are, and the earth, and the things that therein are, and the sea, and the things which are therein, that there should be time no longer: But in the days of the voice of the seventh angel, when he shall begin to sound, the mystery of God should be finished, as he hath declared to his servants the prophets. (Revelation 10:5-7)

Having claimed the earth, Christ now shows that He has full authority over the coming events. He proclaims *that there should be time no longer*, meaning that there will be no further delay. The trumpet of the seventh angel will announce the start of Christ's reign on earth. That His reign is counted before the end of the Great Tribulation shows its inevitability.

And the voice which I heard from heaven spake unto me again, and said, Go and take the little book which is open in the hand of the angel which standeth upon the sea and upon the earth. And I went unto the angel, and said unto him, Give me the little book. And he said unto me, Take it, and eat it up; and it shall make thy belly bitter, but it shall be in thy mouth sweet as honey. And I took the little book out of the angel's hand, and ate it up; and it was in my mouth sweet as honey: and as soon as I had eaten it, my belly was bitter. And he said unto me, Thou must prophesy again before many peoples, and nations, and tongues, and kings. (Revelation 10:8-11)

This [4]little book was a book of prophesy. This revelation of God to John was initially as *sweet as honey* but when the realisation

---

[4]This book is possibly the same one that Daniel was told to *seal...till the time of the end...* (Dan 12:4). It is also mentioned in Dan 12:9. It is worth reading the whole of Daniel chapter 12.

of its contents were fully known to John, his belly was bitter;
the book contained things so appalling, that the knowledge of
them made him feel ill. John is then told that he must continue
to prophesy before *many peoples, and nations, and tongues,
and kings. (Revelation 10:11)*.

11

Revelation chapter 11:
The two witnesses;
the seventh trumpet: the third woe

And there was given me a reed like unto a rod: and the angel stood, saying, Rise, and measure the temple of God, and the altar, and them that worship therein. But the court which is without the temple leave out, and measure it not; for it is given unto the Gentiles: and the holy city shall they tread under foot forty and two months. (Revelation 11:1-2)

Let no man deceive you by any means; for that day shall not come, except there come a falling away first, and that man of sin be revealed, the son of perdition Who opposeth and exalteth himself above all that is called God, or that is worshipped, so that he, as God, sitteth in the temple of God, shewing himself that he is God. (2 Thess 2:3-4)

Revelation 11:1-2 brings to mind that time when the Beast of Revelation chapter 13 will seat himself in the temple at Jerusalem, claim to be God and demand worship. This cannot happen until the church has been removed from the world along with the Holy Spirit, who is the restrainer of evil in the world. This is what is meant by 2 Thessalonians 2:7-8, *For the mystery of iniquity doth already work: only he who now [1]letteth will let,*

---

[1] 'Let' is an old English word meaning to 'hinder'

Revelation chapter 11:
The two witnesses;
the seventh trumpet: the third woe

until he be taken out of the way. And then shall that Wicked be revealed... There is one problem. The Temple at Jerusalem was destroyed by the Romans under Titus in AD70. On that site there now stands a Muslim shrine: the Dome of the Rock, and in what was the outer court, now stands the Al Aqsa Mosque. Before the Beast can seat himself in the temple of God, it will have to be rebuilt. How this can happen is unclear but this Beast to come will be a remarkable man and it is clear from the Bible that this will indeed happen. The Jewish Temple will be rebuilt, [2]Mosaic-style worship will recommence and the Beast will claim to be God, will sit in that rebuilt Temple and demand worship!

And I will give power unto my two witnesses, and they shall prophesy a thousand two hundred and threescore days, clothed in sackcloth. (Revelation 11:3)

The time period quoted is the second 3½ years of the Tribulation period. The period which is called the Great Tribulation. The two witnesses will prophesy *clothed in sackcloth*, a symbol of mourning, because they will identify themselves with Israel's sin and Jerusalem's wickedness (Revelation 11:8). There are two theories about who these two witnesses are:

From Zechariah chapter 4 and Revelation chapter 11 it appears that they are Moses and Elijah, who were seen talking with the Lord while He was [3]transfigured before His disciples:

---

[2]Dan 9:27; 2 Thess 2:3-4

[3]Matthew 17:1-4

124

Revelation chapter 11:
The two witnesses;
the seventh trumpet: the third woe

Zechariah 4:11-14 *What are these two olive trees upon the right side of the [4]candlestick and upon the left side thereof? And I answered again, and said unto him, What be these two olive branches which through the two golden pipes empty the golden [5]oil out of themselves? And he answered me and said, Knowest thou not what these be? And I said, No, my lord. Then said he, These are the two anointed ones, that [6]stand by the Lord of the whole earth.*

Revelation 11:3-4 *And I will give power unto my two witnesses, and they shall prophesy a thousand two hundred and threescore days, clothed in sackcloth. These are the two olive trees, and the two candlesticks standing before the God of the earth.*

Revelation 11:6 *These have power to [7]shut heaven, that it rain not in the days of their prophecy: and have power over [8]waters to turn them to blood, and to smite the earth with all plagues, as often as they will.*

However, some say that since [9]*it is appointed unto men <u>once</u> to die, but after this the judgement*, and because the two witnesses will be [10]killed by the Beast, Moses cannot be one of them

---

[4]The Church (Revelation 1:20)

[5]The two witnesses (anointed ones) are filled with the Holy Spirit, symbolised by the oil.

[6] Moses and Elijah were standing by the Lord at His transfiguration (Mt 17:1-4)

[7]1 Kings 17:1

[8]Exodus 7:19-21

[9]Hebrews 9:27

[10]Revelation 11:7

Revelation chapter 11:
The two witnesses;
the seventh trumpet: the third woe

because he has [11]died once already. If this is the case, the other
possibility is that they are Enoch and Elijah, both of whom
never actually [12]died.

*And when they shall have finished their testimony, the beast that
ascendeth out of the bottomless pit shall make war against them,
and shall overcome them, and kill them. And their dead bodies
shall lie in the street of the great city, which spiritually is called
Sodom and Egypt, where also our Lord was crucified. And they of
the people and kindreds and tongues and nations shall see their
dead bodies three days and an half, and shall not suffer their
dead bodies to be put in graves. And they that dwell upon the
earth shall rejoice over them, and make merry, and shall send
gifts one to another; because these two prophets tormented them
that dwelt on the earth. (Revelation 11:7-10)*

The two witnesses will be able to defend themselves from attack:
Revelation 11:5-6, *And if any man will hurt them, fire proceedeth
out of their mouth, and devoureth their enemies: and if any man
will hurt them, he must in this manner be killed. These have power
to shut heaven, that it rain not in the days of their prophecy: and
have power over waters to turn them to blood, and to smite the
earth with all plagues, as often as they will.* However God will
allow the Beast to *overcome them, and kill them,* but only *when
they shall have finished their testimony (Revelation 11:7).* Their
bodies shall lie in the street of Jerusalem for 3½ days; possibly
this is symbolic of the Great Tribulation period of 3½ years.
Because of the torment wreaked upon them by the two witnesses,
people will rejoice and even send presents to one another, such
will be their joy at seeing them dead.

---

[11]Deuteronomy 34:5-7

[12]Genesis 5:24, 2 Kings 2:11

Revelation chapter 11:
The two witnesses;
the seventh trumpet: the third woe

And after three days and an half the Spirit of life from God entered into them, and they stood upon their feet; and great fear fell upon them which saw them. And they heard a great voice from heaven saying unto them, Come up hither. And they ascended up to heaven in a cloud; and their enemies beheld them. And the same hour was there a great earthquake, and the tenth part of the city fell, and in the earthquake were slain of men seven thousand: and the remnant were affrighted, and gave glory to the God of heaven. (Revelation 11:11-13)

The punishment for their treatment of God's witnesses and for not taking their prophesy to heart will be a great earthquake that will kill 7000 people and destroy one tenth of Jerusalem. Those who remain alive will give *glory to the God of heaven* but not through repentance; it will be through fear!

The second woe is past; and, behold, the third woe cometh quickly. (Revelation 11:14)

The seventh trumpet: the third woe (Revelation 11:15-19)

And the seventh angel sounded; and there were great voices in heaven, saying, The kingdoms of this world are become the kingdoms of our Lord, and of his Christ; and he shall reign for ever and ever. (Revelation 11:15)

The trumpet of the seventh angel announces the beginning of Christ's reign on earth and occurs chronologically close to the end of the Great Tribulation. The vial judgements of Revelation chapter 16 occur soon after the sounding of the seventh angel's trumpet, followed by the second coming of Christ and His victory at the battle of Armageddon (Revelation chapter 19).

Revelation chapter 11:
The two witnesses;
the seventh trumpet: the third woe

And the four and twenty elders, which sat before God on their seats, fell upon their faces, and worshipped God, Saying, We give thee thanks, O Lord God Almighty, which art, and wast, and art to come; because thou hast taken to thee thy great power, and hast reigned. And the nations were angry, and thy wrath is come, and the time of the dead, that they should be judged, and that thou shouldest give reward unto thy servants the prophets, and to the saints, and them that fear thy name, small and great; and shouldest destroy them which destroy the earth.
(Revelation 11:16-18)

It is evident from these verses that the second coming of Christ to reign on earth is certain. It is declared by the 24 elders even while the Beast still reigns upon the earth! The reign of Christ has implications for the ungodly as well as those who love Christ. [13]The dead shall be judged, and God's servants rewarded.

---

[13]It is actually not until the end of Christ's reign upon this earth that the dead will be judged before the great white throne (Revelation 20:11-15). This shows the timelessness of eternity; one thousand years is not a long time for the 24 elders; it is but a moment away! (see 2 Peter 3:8).

Revelation chapter 11:
The two witnesses;
the seventh trumpet: the third woe

And the temple of God was opened in heaven, and there was seen in his temple the ark of his testament: and there were lightnings, and voices, and thunderings, and an earthquake, and great hail. (Revelation 11:19)

The ark of his testament seen within the temple of God speaks of God's faithfulness to His people Israel. This verse is better understood if it is read as the first verse of Revelation chapter 12.

12

Revelation chapter 12:
The future for Israel

And there appeared a great wonder in heaven; a woman clothed with the sun, and the moon under her feet, and upon her head a crown of twelve stars (Revelation 12:1)

The fact that the woman is *clothed with the sun* shows that this is God's chosen people; in Malachi 4:2, Christ is spoken of as *the Sun of righteousness*.

The *moon under her feet* is another indication that the woman portrays Israel, because Israel's times and seasons are governed by the moon. Their's is not a Solar year, but a Lunar year of 354 days, which is 12 lunations of the moon.

If you are still in any doubt as to the woman being Israel, she has *upon her head a crown of twelve stars*; the [1]twelve stars being the twelve tribes of Israel.

---

[1]See Genesis 37:9-10 where the eleven stars in Joseph's dream were understood to represent his eleven brothers. Joseph and his brothers were the sons of Jacob whose name was changed to Israel (Genesis 32:28). The twelve sons of Jacob (Israel) became the twelve tribes of Israel. The tribe of Joseph went by the name of Epraim who was Joseph's second son by his Egyptian wife, Asenath.

And she being with child cried, travailing in birth, and pained to be delivered... And she brought forth a man child, who was to rule all nations with a rod of iron: and her child was caught up unto God, and to his throne. (Revelation 12:2, 5)

The man child is the Lord Jesus Christ, born into the nation of Israel (Mary and Joseph were both descendants of king David). Revelation 12:2 says *And she, being with child, cried, travailing in birth, and pained to be delivered.* Could this refer to Mary, giving birth to Jesus? The time-span that the woman spends in the wilderness (Revelation 12:6) would roughly accord with the time that Mary, Joseph and the young Jesus spent in Egypt after they fled from Herod. The account certainly has a dual nature in parts, and I would not deny that you could read the story of the infant Jesus here. But consider the woman as the Jewish nation, watching and waiting for their Messiah to come. They (Israel) were expectant, they *pained to be delivered* when they were under Roman rule and desperately wanted their Messiah to come, throw out the Romans and rule over them. They were *travailing in birth* when the Lord came and He was not what they expected. Their King was not what they wanted Him to be. They refused to accept Him because He did not come as the warrior king.

And there appeared another wonder in heaven; and behold a great red dragon, having seven heads and ten horns, and seven crowns upon his heads. (Revelation 12:3)

The great red dragon of verse 3 is a complex character: in verse 9 the great dragon symbolises Satan; but in verse 3 the description we are given matches that of the Beast of Revelation chapter 13: he has *seven heads and ten horns, and [2]seven crowns upon his heads*. It would seem that the great red dragon of verse 3 is essentially the embodiment of Satan. In Revelation 13:2, it is apparent that this man, the Beast, is empowered and enthroned by Satan. The dragon and the Beast are two separate entities: hence Revelation 13:4, *they worshipped the dragon who gave power unto the beast; and they worshipped the beast...* – two separate entities. Yet, in Revelation chapter 12:3 the great red dragon has *seven heads and ten horns, and seven crowns upon his heads* – a description of the Beast. Also, Revelation 12:13-17 tells of Satan being hostile toward the Jews, and of course it is ultimately Satan who will do this, but the Jews at that time will see that hostility in the shape of the Beast. [3]Revelation 12:3 is unique in that it unites Satan and the Beast into one being.

[4]Satan's original fall

And his tail drew the third part of the stars of heaven, and did cast them to the earth: and the dragon stood before the woman which

---

[2]Revelation 12:3. In Revelation 13:1 we are told that the Beast has *seven heads and ten horns, and upon his horns ten crowns*. The difference in the number of crowns between Revelation 12:3 and Revelation 13:1 is explained by Daniel 7:7-8 *and behold a fourth beast...and it had ten horns. I considered the horns, and, behold, there came up among them another little horn, before whom there were three of the first horns plucked up by the roots....* 'Horns' in scripture denote authority. Evidently three authorities (kings or governments) tried to go against the Beast and were subdued by him, hence in Revelation 12:3, almost at the end of the age, three countries were under governments other than their own; hence ten horns and only seven crowns.

[3]See also Chapter 13 under the heading of 'Who is the Beast and where is he from?', where more detail is revealed about the Anti-Christ.

[4]See also: 2 Peter 2:4, Jude 1:6

was ready to be delivered, for to devour her child as soon as it was born. (Revelation 12:4)

This is a brief account of Satan's original fall. He and a third of the angels of Heaven rebelled against God and were banished from Heaven. In Luke 10:18, Jesus testified to this, saying *I beheld Satan as lightning fall from heaven.*

The accuser of our brethren

And I heard a loud voice saying in heaven, Now is come salvation, and strength, and the kingdom of our God, and the power of his Christ: for the accuser of our brethren is cast down, which accused them before our God day and night. And they overcame him by the blood of the Lamb, and by the word of their testimony; and they loved not their lives unto the death. Therefore rejoice, ye heavens, and ye that dwell in them. (Revelation 12:10-12a)

Satan is currently [5]*the prince of this world*. Other titles he has are: [6]*the god of this world*, and the [7]*prince of the power of the air*. Though he is banished from Heaven, he has access to God as *the accuser of our brethren (Revelation 12:10)*: There are many references which point to this work of Satan, indeed the whole of the book of Job is based around this, e.g.:

---

[5] John 12:31; 14:30; 16:11

[6] 2 Corinthians 4:4

[7] Ephesians 2:2

Job 1:8, *the LORD said unto Satan, Hast thou considered my servant Job, that there is none like him in the earth, a perfect and an upright man, one who feareth God, and escheweth evil?*

Satan's reply in Job 1:9-11, *Then Satan answered the LORD, and said, Doth Job fear God for nought? Hast thou not made an hedge about him, and about his house, and about all that he hath on every side? Thou hast blessed the work of his hands, and his substance is increased in the land. But put forth thine hand now, and touch all that he hath, and he will curse thee to thy face.*

Another example is found in Luke 22:31-34, *the LORD said Simon, Simon, behold, Satan hath desired to have you, that he may sift you as wheat. But I have prayed for thee, that thy faith fail not. And when thou art converted, strengthen thy brethren. And he said unto him, Lord, I am ready to go with thee, both into prison, and to death. And he said, I tell thee, Peter, the cock shall not crow this day, before that thou shalt thrice deny that thou knowest me.*

This is something which Satan is busy doing today. It could be rather a disconcerting thought because no one is perfect, and Satan could accuse anyone before God. Revelation 12:11 says *...they overcame him by the blood of the Lamb*, showing that we have an advocate, or defender, in the Lord Jesus Christ: *...if any man sin, we have an advocate with the Father, Jesus Christ the righteous. (1 John 2:1)*

Satan cast out of the heavenly realm

And there was war in heaven: Michael and his angels fought against the dragon; and the dragon fought and his angels, And prevailed not; neither was their place found any more in heaven. And the great dragon was cast out, that old serpent, called the

Devil, and Satan, which deceiveth the whole world: he was cast out into the earth, and his angels were cast out with him. And I heard a loud voice saying in heaven, Now is come salvation, and strength, and the kingdom of our God, and the power of his Christ: for the accuser of our brethren is cast down, which accused them before our God day and night. (Revelation 12:7-10)

At present Satan has been banished from Heaven but still has access to God as *the accuser of our brethren*. Revelation 12:7-10 is halfway through the seven year tribulation period: the point at which the Great Tribulation starts, and we find that Satan is cast out of the heavenly realm altogether. [8]Satan will then have just 3½ years of freedom left, hence Revelation 12:12b, *...Woe to the inhabiters of the earth and of the sea! For the devil is come down unto you, having great wrath, because he knoweth that he hath but a short time.* Satanic power is clearly in evidence in the earth during the Great Tribulation!

---

[8]Daniel 9:27, *And he* [the Beast] *shall confirm the covenant with many for one week* [a 'week of years', i.e. seven years]*: and in the midst of the week he shall cause the sacrifice and the oblation to cease, and for the overspreading of abominations he shall make it desolate, even until the consummation, and that determined* [God's judgement] *shall be poured upon the desolate* [lit. desolator, i.e. the Beast]. See also Daniel 7:25

The Jews persecuted

And when the dragon saw that he was cast unto the earth, he persecuted the woman which brought forth the man child. (Revelation 12:13)

After being *cast unto the earth*, Satan, acting through the Beast, will turn against the Jews. This is the time that the Lord Jesus spoke of in Matthew 24:15-16; 21, *When ye, therefore, shall see the abomination of desolation, spoken of by Daniel the prophet stand in the holy place (whosoever readeth let him understand). Then let them who are in Judaea flee into the mountains. For then shall be great tribulation, such as was not since the beginning of the world to this time, no, nor ever shall be.*

More detail is found in 2 Thess 2:3-4, *Let no man deceive you by any means; for that day* [the day of the Lord] *shall not come, except there come a falling away first, and that man of sin be revealed, the son of perdition* [other names for the Beast]. *Who opposeth and exalteth himself above all that is called God, or that is worshipped, so that he, as God, sitteth in the temple of God, shewing himself that he is God.* There is even more detail in Revelation chapter 13 which is dealt with in chapter 13 of this book.

[9]The Jews flee

And the woman fled into the wilderness, where she hath a place prepared of God, that they should feed her there a thousand two hundred and threescore days. And to the woman were given two

---

[9]Compare Zechariah 14:1-8. Could this be the Jews' passage way to the *place prepared by God*?

wings of a great eagle, that she might fly into the wilderness, into her place, where she is nourished for a time, and times, and half a time, from the face of the serpent. And the serpent cast out of his mouth water as a flood after the woman, that he might cause her to be carried away of the flood. And the earth helped the woman, and the earth opened her mouth, and swallowed up the flood which the dragon cast out of his mouth (Revelation 12:6, 14-16)

The Jews will flee from the Beast to *a place prepared by God* where God will protect and sustain them for the remaining 3½ years of the tribulation period. It appears from verses 15-16 that the nation of Israel is pursued by hostile Gentile nations (symbolised by the [10]flood), but that the Jews are protected by other nations who are friendly toward them (symbolised by the earth). Whether this event will be that of physical warfare or whether it will be a political stand-off is unclear, but whichever it is, the Jews will remain safe, ultimately under God's protection.

By this time the church is already translated

It is a comforting thought that Christians will be taken out of the world before the Beast is revealed for who he really is:
2 Thess 2:7 *For the mystery of iniquity doth already work: only he who now letteth* [or hinders] *will let, until he be taken out of the way and then shall that wicked be revealed...*

The One who is restraining evil is the Holy Spirit, indwelling Christians. When He is taken out of the world, at the rapture of the Church, when believers are taken up to be with Christ, evil

---

[10]Compare Daniel 9:26 *the people of the prince that shall come shall destroy the city and the sanctuary, and the end of it shall be with a flood...*

will be unrestrained in the world... *and then shall that wicked* [the Beast] *be revealed.*

Those who come to Christ during the tribulation period are persecuted

And the dragon was wroth with the woman, and went to make war with the remnant of her seed, which keep the commandments of God, and have the testimony of Jesus Christ. (Revelation 12:17)

Angry at being thwarted in his hostility toward Israel, Satan will make war against those who have come to believe in Christ during the tribulation period. Even after the rapture of the church, God will be eager for those remaining on the earth to believe in the Lord Jesus Christ, and so, even though we are told in [11]2 Thess 2:11-12 that *...God shall send them strong delusion, that they should believe a lie* [the lies of the Beast]*: That they all might be damned who believed not the truth, but had pleasure in unrighteousness,* He will send the Holy Spirit back into the world after the translation of the Church, in the form of His [12]two witnesses. Revelation 11:3 says *And I will give power unto my two witnesses, and they shall prophesy a thousand two hundred and threescore days, clothed in sackcloth.*

---

[11]Revelation 12:17 (Jews), Revelation 7:9,14 (Gentiles): Both Jews and Gentiles will be saved during the tribulation period through the preaching of the two witnesses. Those who are saved will see through the lies of the Beast *...God shall send them strong delusion, that they should believe a lie* [the lies of the Beast] (2 Thess 2:11).

[12]The 144000 Jews of Revelation chapters 7 and 14 will also witness during the tribulation period. See chapter 7 for further details on this point.

Satan will turn his wrath upon those who are saved at this time. Even in these perilous times, God will have His representatives on the earth that people may be saved right up to the end.

13

Revelation chapter 13:
All about the Beast

And I stood upon the sand of the sea, and saw a beast rise up out of the sea, having seven heads and ten horns, and upon his horns ten crowns, and upon his heads the name of blasphemy. (Revelation 13:1)

First sight of the Beast! Why will the world choose him?

John, in his vision, *stood upon the sand of the sea*. Used here are two symbols of the world. The [1]sand denotes the vastness of the world population. The sea symbolises the tempestuous nature of the world political scene. John saw a beast *rise up out of the sea*. In other words, this beast will emerge out of a [2]troubled political situation.

When the Beast first makes his appearance, he will come as a peacemaker. He will appear to have genuine solutions to the world's problems at a time of great political turmoil. The Beast will emerge from this turmoil as the man with all the answers and will be swept to power by a world that will find it hard to resist such a man.

---

[1]For example: Genesis 22:17, 32:12, 41:49; Revelation 20:8.

[2]Compare Isaiah 57:20.

And the beast which I saw was like unto a leopard, and his feet were as the feet of a bear, and his mouth as the mouth of a lion (Revelation 13:2)

This is a description analogous to a dream of Daniel. He dreamt about four beasts. In Daniel 7:17 we are told that *These great beasts, which are four, are four kings, which shall arise out of the earth.* The four beasts represent the four empires of the world. The empire of the Beast is described using the same animals: the leopard, bear and lion, as those that Daniel dreamed of and thus will have all the qualities of the empires that went before it. Let us take a brief look at these four beasts of Daniel's dream:

The first was like a lion, and had eagle's wings: I beheld till the wings thereof were plucked, and it was lifted up from the earth, and made stand upon the feet as a man, and a man's heart was given to it. (Daniel 7:4)

The first beast was like a lion, the national symbol of ancient Babylon. This lion had eagles wings and the wings were plucked. The wings of an eagle speak of might and power. The might and power of Babylon was overthrown by the Medes and Persians.

And behold another beast, a second, like to a bear, and it raised up itself on one side, and it had three ribs in the mouth of it between the teeth of it: and they said thus unto it, Arise, devour much flesh. (Daniel 7:5)

The empire of the Medes and Persians is represented by this bear. A bear speaks of savage, brute strength. The three ribs in its mouth probably represent Babylon, Media and Persia, all of which were represented in this second world empire. The devouring of much flesh speaks of the cruelty exercised by this empire in order to reach the peak of world power.

After this I beheld, and lo another, like a leopard, which had upon the back of it four wings of a fowl; the beast had also four heads; and dominion was given to it. (Daniel 7:6)

The leopard is known for its swiftness and speaks of the speed of Alexander the Great's conquests. The four wings of a fowl emphasise this swiftness. Alexander the Great and his armies took only a few months to overthrow the empire of the Medes and Persians. The four heads represent Alexander the Great's four generals among whom the empire was divided after his death.

After this I saw in the night visions, and behold a fourth beast, dreadful and terrible, and strong exceedingly; and it had great iron teeth: it devoured and brake in pieces, and stamped the residue with the feet of it: and it was diverse from all the beasts that were before it; and it had ten horns. (Daniel 7:7)

This fourth beast represents the old Roman empire. This was indeed an [3]iron empire. It had great strength and power and devoured much of the earth with its great iron teeth.

The ten horns of the Beast

There is an aspect here which did not apply to the old Roman empire: *it had ten horns* (Daniel 7:7; Revelation 13:1). The ten horns are in the future. The old Roman empire was never

---

[3]This corresponds perfectly to Nebuchadnezzar's dream in Daniel chapter 2 which also described the fourth empire as iron (Daniel 2:31-33, 40-43).

conquered: it disintegrated, but it will be restored. This time it will have ten horns. Its restored form will be an amalgamation of ten nations or strongholds from the area of the old Roman empire. These ten nations are represented by the ten horns of Daniel 7:7 and Revelation 13:1, and by the ten toes of the image in Nebuchadnezzar's dream in Daniel 2:33, 40-43. These ten nations will form an empire, which will be in existence before the Beast comes to power, as shown in Daniel 7:24: *And the ten horns out of this kingdom are ten kings that shall arise: <u>and another shall rise after them</u>; and he shall be diverse from the first, and he shall [4]subdue three kings.*

This last horn, or king, who will arise is the Beast of Revelation 13:1 and is called the little horn in Daniel 7:8: *I considered the horns, and, behold, there came up among them another little horn, before whom there were three of the first horns plucked up by the roots: and, behold, in this horn were eyes like the eyes of man, and a mouth speaking great things.*

Revelation 17:12-13 also speaks of this: *And the ten horns which thou sawest are ten kings, which have received no kingdom as yet; but receive power as kings one hour with the beast. These have one mind, and shall give their power and strength unto the beast.*

The seven heads of the Beast

The Beast will have *seven heads... (Revelation 13:1)*. This is a reference to Rome. *...The seven heads are seven [5]mountains...*

---

[4]See the note on Revelation 12:3 in chapter 12.

[5]Rome is built on seven hills. It will become more apparent that the seven heads refer to Rome when we consider Revelation chapter 17.

(Revelation 17:9). This is another indication that the empire of the Beast will be a restored form of the old Roman empire. Speaking of Rome, Revelation 17:10 goes on to say: *And there are seven kings: five are fallen, and one is, and the other is not yet come; and when he cometh, he must continue a short space.* These *seven kings* are seven forms of government of the old Roman empire. *five are fallen,* meaning that there had been five forms of government before John wrote these words; *one is:* the sixth form, the imperial form under Julius Caesar, was ruling at the time that John was writing. The Roman empire then declined and appeared to die: Revelation 13:3 *And I saw one of his heads as it were wounded to death; and his deadly wound was healed.*

Notice that one of his heads was <u>*as it were*</u> *wounded to death.* It only <u>appeared</u> to die. The Roman empire has remained in fragmentary form as separate countries, e.g. Britain, Germany etc. This is the seventh form. It was the imperial form of the Roman empire that was *as it were wounded to death.* That wound will be healed when the Beast comes to power (Revelation 13:3). The imperial form of government will exist once more. The Roman empire will be restored. The reign of the Beast will be the eighth form of government: *And the beast that was, and is not, even he is the eighth, and is of the seven... (Revelation 17:11).*

This explains Revelation 17:8 *...the beast that was, and is not, and yet is.* The Roman empire was in existence; now it does not properly exist; and when the Beast comes to power it will exist again.

And they worshipped the dragon which gave power unto the beast: and they worshipped the beast, saying, Who is like unto the beast? who is able to make war with him? (Revelation 13:4)

And all that dwell upon the earth shall worship him, whose names are not written in the book of life of the Lamb slain from the foundation of the world. (Revelation 13:8)

Mankind has always admired strong charismatic leaders. The leadership of the old Roman empire was continually beset by uprisings from conquered nations, and political and religious enemies. Despite this, the majority of people found life more tolerable under Roman rule than they did before. The reason was the 'Pax Romana' or the Roman Peace. The Romans were dealing with the troublemakers and trying to establish peace throughout their empire. People felt safe under Roman rule and were grateful. As a result, the emperor of Rome began to be regarded as divine and people started to worship him. Soon this voluntary emperor worship was enforced and every Roman citizen had to burn a pinch of incense and say 'Caesar is Lord'. The same desire for law and order, security, and freedom from war will be prevalent before the Beast begins his rule. People will willingly swear their allegiance to this man who will promise them peace. Because the Beast's power comes from Satan, any worship of the Beast is worship of Satan himself!

And there was given unto him a mouth speaking great things and blasphemies; and power was given unto him to continue forty and two months. And he opened his mouth in blasphemy against God, to blaspheme his name, and his tabernacle, and them that dwell in heaven. And it was given unto him to make war with the saints, and to overcome them: and power was given him over all kindreds, and tongues, and nations. (Revelation 13:5-7)

The forty two months is the first half of the tribulation period. During this time the Beast blasphemes *against God... and them that dwell in heaven.* Why would the Beast blaspheme those who dwell in Heaven? Christians will be [6]raptured before the Beast is revealed. Therefore the Beast will have to explain how and why millions of Christians are suddenly missing from the world. He will have to discredit the Christian belief and somehow explain this phenomenon away. If it seems incredible that the world will believe him, remember that the Holy Spirit, will have been removed from the world along with the church, and of the remaining inhabitants of the world, the Bible says: *God shall send them strong delusion, that they should believe a lie (2 Thessalonians 2:11).* The Beast will not find it hard to deceive the world. How is the Beast going to make war with the saints when they are gone (raptured) from the world? The saints in Revelation 13:7 are those who will come to Christ during the tribulation period. After the church has been removed from the world, there will be [7]144,000 Jews, who will finally believe that Jesus Christ really is the Messiah. These Jews will take over from the, now raptured, church in [8]proclaiming the gospel.

---

[6]1 Cor 15:50-54, 1 Thess 4:13-17, 2 Thess 2:7

[7]See chapter 7 for more details of the 144,000.

[8]God's two witnesses will also play a part in proclaiming the gospel: see chapter 11.

There will be a great number of converts from their preaching (Revelation 7:9, 14). Among these there will undoubtedly be those who previously regarded themselves as Christians but who will be left behind at the rapture. These may well see their mistakes and turn to Christ in true repentance at this late hour! However, the Beast will *make war* with these tribulation period Christians and will *overcome them*. They will have to make a choice: to worship the Beast or be martyred (Revelation 13:15)!

If any man have an ear, let him hear. He that leadeth into captivity shall go into captivity: he that killeth with the sword must be killed with the sword. Here is the patience and the faith of the saints. (Revelation 13:9-10)

The words *If any man have an ear, let him hear* mean that this is something important that we should try to understand.

He that leadeth into captivity is the Beast and those in authority with him. [9]The false prophet, who is introduced as *another beast* in Revelation 13:11 plays a large part in this. He will lead the people of the world into captivity by causing them to receive the mark of the Beast (Revelation 13:16,17). Those who worship the Beast or receive his mark are condemned to Hell (Revelation 14:11).

He that killeth with the sword is likewise the Beast and those in authority with him. Again, we are told that the false prophet is the instigator of this (Revelation 13:15). He will *cause that as many as would not worship the image of the beast should be killed*.

---

[9]This man is called the 'false prophet' in Revelation 16:13; 19:20; 20:10.

The second reference to the sword in Revelation 13:10: ...*must be killed with the sword* refers to the [10]sword of Jesus Christ, which goes out of His mouth. The sword of the Lord Jesus Christ is His word. He only needs to speak and it is done!

The patience and the faith of the saints is to have the faith that Jesus Christ will return to defeat the Beast and his armies at the battle of [11]Armageddon; that He will indeed tread *the winepress of the fierceness and wrath of Almighty God (Revelation 19:15)*, and to have the patience to await His coming: *...avenge not yourselves, but rather give place unto wrath: for it is written, Vengeance is mine; I will repay, saith the Lord (Romans 12:19).* Christians who are in the world during the tribulation period must obey the (Beast's) law except when it goes against the law of God, that is, worship of the Beast and his image, receiving his mark, etc. They must be prepared to die for their faith [12](Revelation 13:15).

And I beheld another beast coming up out of the earth; and he had two horns like a lamb, and he spake as a dragon. (Revelation 13:11)

This second beast is called the false prophet in Revelation 16:13; 19:20 and 20:10. He comes *out of the earth*. Unlike the Antichrist Beast who comes *up out of the sea* of a troubled political situation, the false prophet will come *out of the earth*. In other words he will come out of a well-established, stable environment. Horns in the Bible denote authority. The false prophet has two horns, therefore he has two spheres of

---

[10]Revelation 19:15, 21; 2 Thess 2:8; Revelation 1:16; Isaiah 11:4.

[11]Revelation 16:13-16; 19:19-21.

[12]See also Revelation 14:9-13.

authority. He is associated with the first (Antichrist) Beast and derives his political authority from him (in Revelation 13:16, 17 he causes people *to receive a mark in their right hand, or in their foreheads... that no man might buy or sell, save he that had the mark'* – political authority; and he causes the world to worship the Antichrist Beast (Revelation 13:12) – Religious authority). Not only does he have two horns but he has *two horns like a lamb*. Jesus Christ is *the Lamb of God (John 1:29)*, and the false prophet appears to be Christ-like. People will see him as someone thoroughly good and trustworthy; but appearances are deceptive because the Bible says *he spake as a dragon*: he is Satanically inspired.

To recap:

- The false prophet will come from a well-established, stable environment.

- He has two spheres of authority.

- He appears Christ-like, but is actually Satanically inspired.

Could this indicate that the false prophet will be a future Pope? Revelation chapters 17 and 18 refer to Rome, as do parts of other chapters. We have already seen how the Beast will be the leader of a restored Roman empire. We have seen that the Beast's seven heads refers to Rome: *...The seven heads are seven [13]mountains... (Revelation 17:9)*. The false prophet has two spheres of authority: political and religious. The Pope has religious authority: the Roman Catholic Church accepts the

---

[13]Rome is built on seven hills. It will become more apparent that the seven heads refer to Rome when we consider Revelation chapter 17.

jurisdiction of the Pope as the supreme head of that church. He also has Political authority: The Pope governs Vatican City and has absolute executive, legislative, and judicial powers within that independent state.

And he **[the false prophet]** *exerciseth all the power of the first beast before him, and causeth the earth and them which dwell therein to worship the first beast, whose deadly wound was healed. And he doeth great wonders, so that he maketh fire come down from heaven on the earth in the sight of men, And deceiveth them that dwell on the earth by the means of those miracles which he had power to do in the sight of the beast; saying to them that dwell on the earth, that they should make an image to the beast, which had the wound by a sword, and did live. And he had power to give life unto the image of the beast, that the image of the beast should both speak, and cause that as many as would not worship the image of the beast should be killed. (Revelation 13:12-15)*

The false prophet will exercise Satanic power to cause the world to worship the Beast. He will do this by deceiving people through signs and wonders. For example, he will cause fire to come down from Heaven. This could be the result of Satanic power controlling the elements unhindered by the Holy Spirit; or it could be done by technical means, for example a laser beam 'flame' fired to earth from a satellite.

It appears that the false prophet will have no power of his own, but derives his power from the Beast: *...he had power ...in the sight of the beast*. Without the Beast, presumably the false prophet will be powerless. The false prophet will cause an image of the Beast to be made and, in some way, will give 'life' to this image. The image will speak, demand worship and sentence those who will not worship to death! Do we take this for a Satanic miracle or will it be accomplished technically, satellite television for example? I think the technical answer is too easy and will not impress a world where television is commonplace and where technology is increasingly taken for granted. The Bible clearly states that 'life' will be given to the image. The Greek word used which is translated 'life' in the Authorized Version of the Bible is 'pneuma' which literally means 'wind' or 'spirit'. Many versions of the Bible interpret it as 'breath'. But what is behind the breath? I think the word 'spirit' would be more correct and in fact 'pneuma' is usually translated 'spirit' and is the word used in Holy Spirit, i.e. Holy 'pneuma'. The most likely explanation is that the image will be indwelt by one of Satan's demons.

Then the decree will go out. People will have a choice between worship of the image of the Beast and death!

And he causeth all, both small and great, rich and poor, free and bond, to receive a mark in their right hand, or in their foreheads: And that no man might buy or sell, save he that had the mark, or the name of the beast, or the number of his name.
(Revelation 13:16-17)

The mark of the Beast will consist of either the name of the Beast, or the number of his name. The word 'mark' literally means an 'impressed mark' or an 'engraving'. The mark could therefore be a visible 'brand', or possibly an implanted electronic microchip. Whatever it is, life will be very difficult without it during the tribulation period. People will not be allowed to buy or sell without it.

Here is wisdom. Let him that hath understanding count the number of the beast: for it is the number of a man; and his number is Six hundred threescore and six. (Revelation 13:18)

Six in the Bible is the number of man. The number six shows that although man was made in [14]the image of God, he is flawed by sin. If man were perfect then he would be represented by the number 7, representing divine perfection and completeness.

Three is a number which denotes mystical completeness. The threefold sixes therefore could denote that this is the man whose sin has reached the pinnacle of wickedness.

Who is the Beast and where is he from?

...and the dragon gave him his power, and his seat, and great authority (Revelation 13:2)
The beast that thou sawest was, and is not; and shall ascend out of the bottomless pit, and go into perdition (Revelation 17:8)

The Beast is not only empowered by Satan (Revelation 13:2), but we are told that he will come out of the [15]bottomless pit (Revelation 17:8). This suggests that he will be a demon incarnated. An actual demon from the bottomless pit in the guise of flesh and blood. If this seems hard to believe consider the following explanation:

Matthew 24:37 *But as the days of Noe* [Noah] *were, so shall also the coming of the Son of man be.*

---

[14]See Genesis 1:27

[15]The bottomless pit is a prison for demons. See the note on Luke 8:30-31 in chapter 9.

So the time of the end will have similarities to Noah's time. Let us look at one aspect of this:

Genesis 6:1-4 *And it came to pass, when men began to multiply on the face of the earth, and daughters were born unto them, that the [16]sons of God saw the daughters of men that they were fair; and they took them wives of all which they chose. And the LORD said, My spirit shall not always strive with man, for that he also is flesh: yet his days shall be an hundred and twenty years. There were giants in the earth in those days; and also after that, when the sons of God came in unto the daughters of men, and they bare children to them, the same became mighty men which were of old, men of renown.*

The *Sons of God* were angels (demons) who interbred with the fairest of the daughters of men. Fallen angels assumed human

---

[16]Some take the view that the *sons of God* refers to the Godly line of Seth, and the *daughters of men* to the ungodly line of Cain. Those who hold this view reject the idea that the *sons of God* are angels because of Lk 20:34-36 and Mt 22:30. However, in Lk 20:35 the ones who do not marry are not angels but resurrected saints. Mt 22:30 says of the resurrected saints *they neither marry, nor are given in marriage, but are as the angels of God in heaven.* This says nothing of fallen angels. While it is true that the angels of God in Heaven do not marry, angels are subject to temptation and are thus capable of sin (Job 4:18, Jude 6, 2 Peter 2:4). If the *sons of God* does refer to angels then they would of course be fallen angels and not heavenly angels. The term *sons of God* in this passage is 'bene Elohim' which is consistently used of angels (e.g. Job 1:6, 2:1, 38:7). It could be that it was the inter-marriage of fallen angels with women that was responsible for the *wickedness of man (Gen. 6:5)* and caused God to destroy this inter-bred being with the great flood. The theory of marriage between Godly Sethites with ungodly Cainites fails to account for the 'Nephilim' or *Giants* of Genesis 6:4. The word 'Nephilim' which means 'fallen ones' is only used in Genesis 6:4 and Numbers 13:33 where we are told that they are the *sons of Anak.* 'Anak' means 'Giant' or 'Long necked'. It is interesting that a distinction is made between the *men of a great stature (Numbers 13:32)* and the *giants* (Nephilim – Numbers 13:33). The *giants* appear to be more than just big men!

form and married human women. The result was a race of giant-like 'men'. *But as the days of Noe* [Noah] *were, so shall also the coming of the Son of man be (Matthew 24:37).*

It follows that since the Beast *shall ascend out of the bottomless pit*, he can only be one of the terrible demons imprisoned there. It seems likely, Satan being a great imitator of God, that just as God the Holy Spirit implanted the Lord Jesus Christ into the womb of Mary to produce God incarnate, the Son of God, a person who is both God and man, that Satan will copy this act and will implant one of his demons into a human woman to produce a demon incarnate, a being who is both demon and man. He will then have a proper 'human' background and will not just appear from nowhere.

A simpler explanation is also possible. In the days of Noah, demons assumed human form to marry human women. It is possible that the Beast will simply be a demon in human form.

When will the Beast be revealed?

Let no man deceive you by any means: for that day shall not come, except there come a falling away first, and that man of sin be revealed, the son of perdition... For the mystery of iniquity doth already work: only he who now letteth will let, until he be taken out of the way. And then shall that Wicked be revealed, whom the Lord shall consume with the spirit of his mouth, and shall destroy with the brightness of his coming: Even him, whose coming is after the working of Satan with all power and signs and lying wonders. (2 Thessalonians 2:3,7-9)

...many shall come in my name, saying, I am Christ; and shall deceive many. And ye shall hear of wars and rumours of wars: see that ye be not troubled: for all these things must come to pass,

but the end is not yet. For nation shall rise against nation, and kingdom against kingdom: and there shall be famines, and pestilences, and earthquakes, in divers places... And many false prophets shall rise, and shall deceive many. And because iniquity shall abound, the love of many shall wax cold. But he that shall endure unto the end, the same shall be saved. And this gospel of the kingdom shall be preached in all the world for a witness unto all nations; and then shall the end come...When ye therefore shall see the abomination of desolation, spoken of by Daniel the prophet, stand in the holy place, (whoso readeth, let him understand:) Then let them which be in Judaea flee into the mountains... For then shall be great tribulation, such as was not since the beginning of the world to this time, no, nor ever shall be. And except those days should be shortened, there should no flesh be saved: but for the elect's sake those days shall be shortened. (Matthew 24:5-7,11-16,21,22)

Do we know the timescale any more precisely than this? The angel Gabriel spoke to Daniel (Daniel 9:21-27) and revealed to him the timing of the Beast's advent:

Seventy weeks are determined upon thy people and upon thy holy city, to finish the transgression, and to make an end of sins, and to make reconciliation for iniquity, and to bring in everlasting righteousness, and to seal up the vision and prophecy, and to anoint the most Holy. (Daniel 9:24)

Daniel is told that within seventy weeks, certain things will be accomplished with respect to Israel:

to finish the transgression

The Jews would be freed from their captivity. They were at that time in captivity in Babylon.

to make an end of sins

Atonement would be made for their sins. This atonement came in the form of Jesus Christ.

to make reconciliation for iniquity

The sacrifice of Jesus Christ has effected reconciliation with God.

to bring in everlasting righteousness

Christ will come to reign on this earth for 1000 years.

to seal up the vision and prophecy

But thou, O Daniel, shut up the words, and seal the book, even to the time of the end... (Daniel 12:4)

Our understanding of this will be sealed until the time of the end. An understanding of the end times is a sure sign that the time of the end is drawing near.

to anoint the most Holy

For unto us a child is born, unto us a son is given: and the government shall be upon his shoulder: and his name shall be called Wonderful, Counsellor, The mighty God, The everlasting Father, The Prince of Peace. Of the increase of his government and peace there shall be no end, upon the throne of David, and upon his kingdom, to order it, and to establish it with judgment and with justice from henceforth even for ever. The zeal of the LORD of hosts will perform this. (Isaiah 9:6-7)

The most holy place or the holy of holies will be anointed when Christ returns to rule *upon the throne of David*. Although it was Solomon who built the original [17]temple of Jerusalem, it was David who drew the plans for the temple and who prepared the way for Solomon to build it.

All this was to be accomplished within seventy weeks (Daniel 9:24). The word 'week' is the Hebrew word 'Shabua' which means 'a seven' or 'a week'. This same Hebrew word is used in Genesis 29:27-29 where Jacob worked for Laban seven years for Rachel: *Fulfil her week, and we will give thee this also for the service which thou shalt serve with me yet seven other years*. A week here is a 'week of years' or seven years. The seventy weeks in Daniel 9:24 is really a period of 70 x 7 years, or 490 years.

Know therefore and understand, that from the going forth of the commandment to restore and to build Jerusalem unto the Messiah the Prince shall be seven weeks, and threescore and two weeks: the street shall be built again, and the wall, even in troublous times. And after threescore and two weeks shall Messiah be cut off, but not for himself: and the people of the prince that shall come shall destroy the city and the sanctuary; and the end thereof shall be with a flood, and unto the end of the war desolations are determined. (Daniel 9:25-26)

69 weeks or 483 years of this prophecy have been fulfilled. 1 week or 7 years remain to be fulfilled. Daniel 9:25 says that from the decree to restore and rebuild Jerusalem until the coming of Christ equals *seven weeks, and three score and two weeks*, which is 69 weeks or 483 years. These 483 years started from the decree of Artaxerxes to rebuild Jerusalem, and finished

---

[17]1 Chronicles 22:6-11

with the appearance of Christ riding into Jerusalem on a colt.
The [18]decree was issued in the year 445 BC. From that time until
Jesus rode into Jerusalem on a colt was 483 years. It took
7 weeks or 49 years to rebuild Jerusalem and 62 weeks or
434 years later Jesus rode into Jerusalem and was crucified. At
this point, at the end of the 69th week, at the death of Christ, the
clock has been stopped.

When will the clock restart?

*And he shall confirm the covenant with many for one week: and
in the midst of the week he shall cause the sacrifice and the
oblation to cease, and for the overspreading of abominations he
shall make it desolate, even until the consummation, and that
determined shall be poured upon the desolate. (Daniel 9:27)*

The one who will *confirm the covenant with many* is the Beast of
Revelation chapter 13. He will sign a covenant guaranteeing
protection for Israel and freedom to worship God according to the
law of Judaism. The signing of this covenant will restart the clock.
This is the start of the seven year tribulation period (the final week
of Daniel's prophecy). In the middle of the seven year agreement,
that is, after 3½ years, the Beast will break this covenant and turn
on the [19]Jews: *he shall cause the sacrifice and the oblation to
cease, and for the overspreading of abominations he shall make it
desolate.* [20]He will set himself up as God and demand worship.

---

[18]Nehemiah 2:1-10

[19]See chapter 12 for more detail on this aspect.

[20]2 Thessalonians 2:4

Nobody can specify the time that this 70th week will start. All that can be said is that the 70th week will start when the Beast signs the covenant with Israel. It is important therefore to keep abreast of world events:

Matthew 24:36 *But of that day and hour knoweth no man, no, not the angels of heaven, but my Father only.*

Matthew 25:13 *Watch therefore, for ye know neither the day nor the hour wherein the Son of man cometh.*

14

Revelation chapter 14:
First glimpses – New Jerusalem and Armageddon

And I looked, and, lo, a Lamb stood on the mount Sion, and with him an hundred forty and four thousand, having his Father's name written in their foreheads. (Revelation 14:1)

[1]*Mount Sion* refers not to the mountain forming part of earthly Jerusalem, but to the heavenly city, [2]New Jerusalem. This is evident from Revelation 14:3 – the 144,000 are not on earth, they are before the throne of God. Another proof that *Mount Sion* is New Jerusalem is also found in verse 3: it says they *were redeemed from the earth.* [3]The 144,000 are Jews who come to faith in Christ during the tribulation period. Unlike most on the earth during this time who will worship the Beast and receive his mark *in their right hand, or in their foreheads (Revelation 13:16)*, the 144,000 will have the *Father's name written in their foreheads*.

And I heard a voice from heaven, as the voice of many waters, and as the voice of a great thunder: and I heard the voice of harpers harping with their harps: And they sung as it were a new song before the throne, and before the four beasts, and the elders:

---

[1]Compare Hebrews 12:22

[2]Revelation 3:12, 21:2

[3]See the narrative in chapter 7 for further details on the 144,000.

and no man could learn that song but the hundred and forty and four thousand, which were redeemed from the earth. (Revelation 14:2-3)

> The sound that John heard: *as the voice of many waters and as the voice of a great thunder: and...the voice of harpers harping with their harps* was the sound of a 144,000-strong choir singing *as it were a new song*. The 144,000 will be the only ones who can learn this song.

These are they which were not defiled with women; for they are virgins. These are they which follow the Lamb whithersoever he goeth. These were redeemed from among men, being the firstfruits unto God and to the Lamb. And in their mouth was found no guile: for they are without fault before the throne of God. (Revelation 14:4-5)

> *Women* and *virgins* are not used here in an earthly sense, since *marriage is honourable in all, and the bed undefiled (Hebrews 13:4).*

> The term *women* is used to describe a corrupt false [4]church which practises spiritual fornication.

> *Virgins* is used in the sense of 2 Cor 11:2, *For I am jealous over you with godly jealousy: for I have espoused you to one husband, that I may present you as a chaste virgin to Christ.* The 144,000 have been utterly faithful to their Lord. They have not worshiped the Beast, or practised any other spiritual corruption. They are utterly pure in the spiritual sense.

---

[4]This corrupt false church will be revealed when we look at Revelation chapter 17.

And I saw another angel fly in the midst of heaven, having the everlasting gospel to preach unto them that dwell on the earth, and to every nation, and kindred, and tongue, and people, Saying with a loud voice, Fear God, and give glory to him; for the hour of his judgment is come: and worship him that made heaven, and earth, and the sea, and the fountains of waters...And the third angel followed them, saying with a loud voice, If any man worship the beast and his image, and receive his mark in his forehead, or in his hand, The same shall drink of the wine of the wrath of God, which is poured out without mixture into the cup of his indignation; and he shall be tormented with fire and brimstone in the presence of the holy angels, and in the presence of the Lamb: And the smoke of their torment ascendeth up for ever and ever: and they have no rest day nor night, who worship the beast and his image, and whosoever receiveth the mark of his name. (Revelation 14:6,7, 9-11)

This is the last chance for those on the earth to turn away from the Beast and worship God. In Revelation chapter 13, the false prophet will command those on the earth to worship the Beast. The penalty for not doing so will be death! He will also command that everybody should swear their allegiance to the Beast by having the Beasts's mark indelibly written on their right hand or forehead. Those without the mark of the Beast will not be able to buy or sell. At this point, word comes from God that anyone who worships the Beast or receives his mark will be condemned to everlasting torment in the [5]lake of fire and brimstone. This place is generally known as 'Hell'. For those who worship the Beast or receive his mark there will be no turning back!

---

[5]Revelation 19:20; 20:10; 21:8

The word *angel* used here is translated from the Greek word 'aggelos' which means a 'messenger' or an 'agent'. The 'angels' will actually be the two witnesses of Revelation chapter 11. It is the two witnesses who will preach the gospel on the earth during the reign of the Beast. The church will have been removed (raptured) before the Beast is revealed and so the two witnesses will become God's 'voice' in the earth during this time. When the decree goes out to worship the Beast and to receive his mark, these two witnesses will proclaim the last chance warning to those on the earth to turn from the Beast and not to worship him or receive his mark.

And there followed another angel, saying, Babylon is fallen, is fallen, that great city, because she made all nations drink of the wine of the wrath of her fornication. (Revelation 14:8)

[6]*Babylon* in the book of Revelation is a symbolic name for Rome. To the Jews of this time, the power of Rome was regarded in the same manner as the power of Babylon was to its contemporaries. A comparison of Jeremiah 51:7-8 with Revelation 14:8 will reveal this similarity. In fact the fall of literal Babylon and the fall of symbolic Babylon (Rome) are both represented by Jeremiah chapters 50 and 51.

An angel declares that *Babylon is fallen, is fallen.*

is fallen, is fallen means that Babylon is completely fallen. The fall of both the religious and political aspects of Rome is meant here. This event is described more fully in Revelation chapters 17 and 18.

---

[6]More information on *Babylon* will be found in chapter 17.

...If any man worship the beast and his image, and receive his mark in his forehead, or in his hand, The same shall drink of the wine of the wrath of God, which is poured out without mixture into the cup of his indignation; and he shall be tormented with fire and brimstone in the presence of the holy angels, and in the presence of the Lamb: And the smoke of their torment ascendeth up for ever and ever: and they have no rest day nor night, who worship the beast and his image, and whosoever receiveth the mark of his name. (Revelation 14:9-11)

Those who worship the Beast and his image and receive the mark of the Beast will be [7]tormented in the lake of fire. Their crime is so heinous that the wrath of God will be poured out upon them *without mixture*, i.e. undiluted. Their torment is unceasing: *they have no rest day nor night.* In Luke 16:19-31, those in Hell can see those in Heaven, thus deepening their torment. There is however *a great gulf fixed* (Luke 16:26) so that it is impossible to go from one side to the other.

Here is the patience of the saints: here are they that keep the commandments of God, and the faith of Jesus. And I heard a voice from heaven saying unto me, Write, Blessed are the dead which die in the Lord from henceforth: Yea, saith the Spirit, that they may rest from their labours; and their works do follow them. And I looked, and behold a white cloud, and upon the cloud one sat like unto the Son of man, having on his head a golden crown, and in his hand a sharp sickle. And another angel came out of the temple, crying with a loud voice to him that sat on the cloud, Thrust in thy sickle, and reap: for the time is come for thee to reap; for the harvest of the earth is ripe. And he that sat on the cloud thrust in his sickle on the earth; and the earth was reaped. And another angel came out of the temple which is in heaven, he

---

[7]A more detailed look at Hell will be found in chapter 6.

also having a sharp sickle. And another angel came out from the altar, which had power over fire; and cried with a loud cry to him that had the sharp sickle, saying, Thrust in thy sharp sickle, and gather the clusters of the vine of the earth; for her grapes are fully ripe. And the angel thrust in his sickle into the earth, and gathered the vine of the earth, and cast it into the great winepress of the wrath of God. And the winepress was trodden without the city, and blood came out of the winepress, even unto the horse bridles, by the space of a thousand and six hundred furlongs. (Revelation 14:12-20)

It is the Lord Jesus Christ who sits on the white cloud. The white cloud denotes divine presence and the golden crown indicates the Lord's divine kingship.

This passage refers to the battle of Armageddon which is dealt with more fully in chapter 19. To set the scene, the events leading up to this battle are outlined below:

- The church will have been removed from the world.

- The Beast of Revelation chapter 13 will be world dictator.

- Because the church will have been removed, the Holy Spirit will not be there to restrain evil in the world. The world will deteriorate so fast under the Beast's evil rule that Jesus said in Matthew 24:22: *except those days should be shortened, there should no flesh be saved...*

- The rule of the Beast will be shortened by the Lord Jesus Christ and His heavenly army at the battle of Armageddon.

The emphasis in this chapter is on the timing of this event. If mankind carried on under the rule of the Beast, the whole world

would be destroyed, probably by nuclear war. This is implied
by Jesus' statement in Matthew 24:22: *except those days should
be shortened, there should no flesh be saved....* At this time the
sins of the world will be fully developed, ready for God's
judgement. This is indicated in Revelation 14:18 where an angel
says: *Thrust in thy sharp sickle, and gather the clusters of the
vine of the earth; for her grapes are fully ripe.*

The first reaping in Revelation 14:15-16 however, is that of the
Godly harvest: *And another angel came out of the temple,
crying with a loud voice to him that sat on the cloud, Thrust in
thy sickle, and reap: for the time is come for thee to reap; for
the harvest of the earth is ripe. And he that sat on the cloud
thrust in his sickle on the earth; and the earth was reaped.*
Those who have turned to Christ during the tribulation period,
and have survived until this time are protected from the wrath of
God which is poured out upon the Beast and his armies at the
battle of Armageddon.

The second reaping (Revelation 14:19) is the battle of
Armageddon itself. The time is right for the crop of evil to be
reaped: *...her grapes are fully ripe.* This second reaping is
performed by an angel who has power over fire, symbolising a
cleansing of the earth. The *winepress of the wrath of God*
signifies the shedding of sinners' blood. This blood will be shed
outside the city. All uncleanness is disposed of [8]outside the
borders of the city. The quantity of shed blood is described as
coming up to the horses bridles for an distance of 1600 furlongs
or 200 miles! We are told the length and height of this stream of
blood but we are not told the width; therefore it is impossible to
calculate how many people are slain at the battle of
Armageddon with any accuracy. However an approximation

---

[8] e.g. Leviticus 14:40-45

based on the stream being just three feet wide gives a figure of 50 million people. At the other end of the scale, if we assume that the stream will be the same average width as the River Thames (which is approximately the same length) we get a figure of 160,000 million people. The true figure is probably somewhere between these two extremes.

15

Revelation chapter 15:
Preparation for the seven last plagues

And I saw another sign in heaven, great and marvellous, seven
angels having the seven last plagues; for in them is filled up the
wrath of God. (Revelation 15:1)

This sign that John sees, shows that God's wrath upon the
tribulation period earth is not spontaneous, but is planned and
measured. [1]God knows how the world will develop and has had
this end-time wrath prepared in advance.

And I saw as it were a sea of glass mingled with fire: and them
that had gotten the victory over the beast, and over his image, and
over his mark, and over the number of his name, stand on the sea
of glass, having the harps of God. And they sing the song of
Moses the servant of God, and the song of the Lamb, saying,
Great and marvellous are thy works, Lord God Almighty; just and
true are thy ways, thou King of saints. Who shall not fear thee, O
Lord, and glorify thy name? for thou only art holy: for all nations
shall come and worship before thee; for thy judgments are made
manifest. (Revelation 15:2-4)

Tribulation period martyrs are depicted here. The *sea of glass*
mingled with fire contrasts the stability and tranquillity of
Heaven, their new abode with the instability and persecution

---

[1]Isaiah 46:10

they suffered on the earth at the hands of the Beast. [2]These tribulation period believers had refused to worship the Beast and his image and had refused to bear the mark of the Beast. These now play the harps of God and sing the song of Moses and the song of the Lamb.

And after that I looked, and, behold, the temple of the tabernacle of the testimony in heaven was opened: And the seven angels came out of the temple, having the seven plagues, clothed in pure and white linen, and having their breasts girded with golden girdles. And one of the four beasts gave unto the seven angels seven golden vials full of the wrath of God, who liveth for ever and ever. And the temple was filled with smoke from the glory of God, and from his power; and no man was able to enter into the temple, till the seven plagues of the seven angels were fulfilled. (Revelation 15:5-8)

Unlike the former judgements which come from God's throne, these final judgements come from God's temple. The seven angels are *clothed in pure and white linen, and having their breasts girded with golden girdles*, representing the holiness of their mission. The golden vials represent sacrifical offerings to appease a God who is offended by the Beast and those who worship him. The golden vials were temple vessels used to pour

---

[2]Revelation 13:4, 14-17

out [3]drink offerings to God. The number seven depicts that these final judgements are the complete wrath of God poured out on the earth at this time.

---

[3]There are numerous references to drink offerings in the Old Testament, e.g. Leviticus 23:13

16

Revelation chapter 16:
The seven last plagues

These seven last plagues are events which happen before *the earth was reaped* as described in Revelation 14:14-20, and continue to the end of the tribulation period. They culminate in the second coming of the Lord Jesus Christ in victory at the battle of Armageddon.

The command and the first judgement vial (Revelation 16:1-2)

And I heard a great voice out of the temple saying to the seven angels, Go your ways, and pour out the vials of the wrath of God upon the earth. And the first went, and poured out his vial upon the earth; and there fell a noisome and grievous sore upon the men which had the mark of the beast, and upon them which worshipped his image. (Revelation 16:1-2)

The command of God from Heaven indicates that God's [1]long-suffering is over. Now, the wrath of God is poured out upon the earth. The judgement that He has been [2]withholding, will finally be unleashed.

---

[1]2 Peter 3:9

[2]See the preamble to chapter 6 for information on God's judgement delayed.

The first angel pours out his vial upon the earth, which at this time will be under the leadership of the Beast. The judgement of God upon those *which had the mark of the beast and...which worshipped his image* is *a noisome and grievous sore.* This could well be a widespread and virulent cancer due to the [3]climatic changes that take place upon the earth during the tribulation period. It is implied that those who have come to trust Christ during the tribulation period will be protected from this judgement because we are told that the judgement will fall *upon the men which had the mark of the beast, and upon them which worshipped his image.*

Vials two and three (Revelation 16:3-7)

And the second angel poured out his vial upon the sea; and it became as the blood of a dead man: and every living soul died in the sea. And the third angel poured out his vial upon the rivers and fountains of waters; and they became blood. And I heard the angel of the waters say, Thou art righteous, O Lord, which art, and wast, and shalt be, because thou hast judged thus. For they have shed the blood of saints and prophets, and thou hast given them blood to drink; for they are worthy. And I heard another out of the altar say, Even so, Lord God Almighty, true and righteous are thy judgments. (Revelation 16:3-7)

These are devastating judgements that God pours out upon a largely unregenerate and ungrateful tribulation period world. Both the sea and all fresh water will literally become blood and

---

[3]See chapter 8. It would in no way lessen the fact that this is a judgement from God if it is caused by 'natural' means. God frequently uses natural events as judgements. For example, God has often used other nations to punish Israel, in fact the whole book of Ezekiel is an example of this.

every creature in the sea will die. This judgement is the direct result of the Beast [4]killing all who will not worship him and his image, and for killing God's two witnesses (prophets). The judgement may also take in the martyrs throughout the church age too, thus answering the prayer of those under the altar in Revelation 6:9-11: *And when he had opened the fifth seal, I saw under the altar the souls of them that were slain for the word of God, and for the testimony which they held: And they cried with a loud voice, saying, How long, O Lord, holy and true, dost thou not judge and avenge our blood on them that dwell on the earth? And white robes were given unto every one of them; and it was said unto them, that they should rest yet for a little season, until their fellowservants also and their brethren, that should be killed as they were, should be fulfilled.* The Beast and his subjects are given blood to drink instead of water because that is what they are worthy of.

Those who have accepted Christ as their Lord and Saviour during the tribulation period will, however, be excluded from this judgement:

Revelation 12:6 *And the woman fled into the wilderness, where she hath a place prepared of God, that they should feed her there a thousand two hundred and threescore days.*

Revelation 12:14 *And to the woman were given two wings of a great eagle, that she might fly into the wilderness, into her place, where she is nourished for a time, and times, and half a time, from the face of the serpent.*

The 'woman' in Revelation chapter 12 are those Jews in Israel who will refuse to worship the Beast. These will heed God's

---

[4]Revelation 13:11-15 and Revelation 11:3-7.

word, having [5]recognised the Beast for who he is, and will do
that which God has [6]commanded them to do.

The fourth vial (Revelation 16:8-9)

*And the fourth angel poured out his vial upon the sun; and power
was given unto him to scorch men with fire. And men were
scorched with great heat, and blasphemed the name of God,
which hath power over these plagues: and they repented not to
give him glory. (Revelation 16:8-9)*

I will repeat here part of that which I have written in chapter 8.
Revelation chapters 8 and 16 are very closely linked. The
judgements of chapter 16 are linked to the events described in
chapter 8.

*And the fourth angel sounded, and the third part of the sun was
smitten, and the third part of the moon, and the third part of the
stars; so as the third part of them was darkened, and the day
shone not for a third part of it, and the night likewise.
(Revelation 8:12)*

*And the fourth angel poured out his vial upon the sun; and power
was given unto him to scorch men with fire. And men were
scorched with great heat... (Revelation 16:8-9)*

*Behold, the day of the LORD cometh, cruel both with wrath and
fierce anger... For the stars of heaven and the constellations*

---

[5]e.g. Daniel 9:26-27

[6]Matthew 24:15-22

thereof shall not give their light: the sun shall be darkened in his going forth, and the moon shall not cause her light to shine. Therefore I will shake the heavens, and the earth shall remove out of her place, in the wrath of the LORD of hosts, and in the day of his fierce anger. (Isaiah 13:9,10,13)

It seems that after the fourth angel has sounded his trumpet the earth will no longer have a 24 hour day but a 16 hour day (Revelation 8:12). We are told that it is also the fourth angel who *poured out his vial upon the sun; and power was given unto him to scorch men with fire (Revelation 16:8)*. Since both of these events are the work of the fourth angel, it is likely that they both happen at the same time. We have seen in Revelation chapter 8 that there is going to be great calamity upon the earth. I have put forward the idea that the main catastrophe could be the fall of a giant meteorite, perhaps hundreds of miles in diameter. This would totally change the earth as we know it. Weather patterns would be upset and there would be mass death and destruction. It also seems feasible that a collision with such a large meteorite would knock the earth into a new orbit slightly closer to the sun (Revelation 16:8-9). This could explain how men become *scorched with great heat (Revelation 16:9)*. Such an occurrence could also increase the speed that the earth spins on its axis, shortening the day to 16 hours. This would fulfil Isaiah's prophecy: *Therefore I will shake the heavens, and the earth shall remove out of her place, in the wrath of the LORD of hosts, and in the day of his fierce anger. (Isaiah 13:13)*.

However, such is the stubbornness of man that despite these judgements of God they *blasphemed the name of God, which hath power over these plagues: and they repented not to give him glory. (Revelation 16:9)*

The fifth vial (Revelation 16:10-11)

And the fifth angel poured out his vial upon the seat of the beast; and his kingdom was full of darkness; and they gnawed their tongues for pain, And blasphemed the God of heaven because of their pains and their sores, and repented not of their deeds. (Revelation 16:10-11)

This judgement is concentrated *upon the seat* [throne] *of the beast*. The word 'darkness' literally means 'to be darkened'. Whether this darkness is literal or spiritual or both is unclear. Some Bible translations, interpret the word 'pain' as 'anguish'; the literal translation is 'labour'. Again, it is unclear whether they *gnawed their tongues* for physical pain or whether the 'pain' is mental, i.e. anguish or stress. Whichever way we are supposed to take this judgement, one thing is clear, they still remain stubbornly opposed to God. They *blasphemed the God of heaven because of their pains and their sores, and repented not of their deeds.*

The sixth vial: preparation for the battle of Armageddon

And the sixth angel poured out his vial upon the great river Euphrates; and the water thereof was dried up, that the way of the kings of the east might be prepared. And I saw three unclean spirits like frogs come out of the mouth of the dragon, and out of the mouth of the beast, and out of the mouth of the false prophet. For they are the spirits of devils, working miracles, which go forth unto the kings of the earth and of the whole world, to gather them to the battle of that great day of God Almighty. Behold, I come as a thief. Blessed is he that watcheth, and keepeth his garments, lest he walk naked, and they see his shame. And he gathered them together into a place called in the Hebrew tongue Armageddon. (Revelation 16:12-16)

The sixth vial sets the scene for the battle of Armageddon. Revelation chapter 19 gives us details of the battle itself.

The Euphrates river has its source in the Armenian mountains. Its water is chiefly sustained by the annual melting of snow in the Armenian highlands. The sixth judgement vial involves the drying up of the Euphrates river; a river that is 1780 miles long and 400 yards wide at its widest point. How could this great river become dried up? It is possible that the earth's hotter climate due to God's previous [7]judgements will be the cause of the drying up of the Euphrates river. It is dried up so that *the way of the kings of the east might be prepared.* These are countries to the east of the Euphrates river who will be gathered to the battle of Armageddon by Satan. We are told that *three unclean spirits like frogs come out of the mouth of the dragon* [Satan], *and out of the mouth of the beast, and out of the mouth of the false prophet. For they are the spirits of devils, working*

---

[7]See narrative on The fourth vial (Revelation 16:8-9) above

179

miracles, which go forth unto the kings of the earth and of the whole world, to gather them to the battle of that great day of God Almighty [Armageddon]. It is not just the kings of the east who are incited to war, although the Euphrates is dried up specifically for them, but it is the whole world, all of those who are under the beast's rule will be drawn into this area. Whatever pretext they are given for this invasion, the Bible makes it quite clear that they are there to wage war on Christ and His army: *And I saw the beast, and the kings of the earth, and their armies, gathered together to make war against him that sat on the horse* [Christ], *and against his army* [raptured Christians]. *(Revelation 19:19).*

During the tribulation period, Christians are encouraged to be faithful until Christ's return. Just as the Beast and his armies will be surprised by the suddenness of Christ's appearance at Armageddon, so will Christ's followers. They are given encouragement to persevere. Christ says of His coming: *Behold, I come as a thief. Blessed is he that watcheth, and keepeth his garments, lest he walk naked, and they see his shame (Revelation 16:15).*

The seventh vial (Revelation 16:17-21)

And the seventh angel poured out his vial into the air; and there came a great voice out of the temple of heaven, from the throne, saying, It is done. And there were voices, and thunders, and lightnings; and there was a great earthquake, such as was not since men were upon the earth, so mighty an earthquake, and so great. And the great city was divided into three parts, and the cities of the nations fell: and great Babylon came in remembrance before God, to give unto her the cup of the wine of the fierceness of his wrath. And every island fled away, and the mountains were not found. And there fell upon men a great hail out of heaven, every stone about the weight of a talent: and men blasphemed

*God because of the plague of the hail; for the plague thereof was
exceeding great. (Revelation 16:17-21)*

The great voice from the temple of Heaven declaring *it is done*
announces the completion of God's wrath upon the earth. Since
the flood there has never been such devastation on the earth.
There is thunder and lightning and a huge earthquake which
affects the whole world! [8]*The great city is split into three parts,*
and *the cities of the nations fell*, meaning cities worldwide.
every island fled away, and the mountains were not found, i.e.
whole islands are destroyed without trace and mountains are
demolished. This will be a colossal earthquake which will cause
massive worldwide destruction. Following these events will
come a hailstorm with hailstones weighing about 100 pounds
each *and men blasphemed God because of the plague of the
hail; for the plague thereof was exceeding great.*

*and great Babylon came in remembrance before God, to give
unto her the cup of the wine of the fierceness of his wrath.*
Revelation chapters 17 and 18 deal with God's judgement upon
'Babylon' which is a continuation of the seventh judgement
vial.

---

[8]In the book of Revelation, the great city is either Jerusalem or 'Babylon' , i.e.
Rome (this will become apparent when we consider Revelation chapter 17). It is
probably Rome which is meant here.

17

Revelation chapter 17:
The great whore of Babylon

And there came one of the seven angels which had the seven vials, and talked with me, saying unto me, Come hither; I will shew unto thee the judgment of the great whore that sitteth upon many waters: With whom the kings of the earth have committed fornication, and the inhabitants of the earth have been made drunk with the wine of her fornication. So he carried me away in the spirit into the wilderness: and I saw a woman sit upon a scarlet coloured beast, full of names of blasphemy, having seven heads and ten horns. And the woman was arrayed in purple and scarlet colour, and decked with gold and precious stones and pearls, having a golden cup in her hand full of abominations and filthiness of her fornication: And upon her forehead was a name written, MYSTERY, BABYLON THE GREAT, THE MOTHER OF HARLOTS AND ABOMINATIONS OF THE EARTH. And I saw the woman drunken with the blood of the saints, and with the blood of the martyrs of Jesus: and when I saw her, I wondered with great admiration. (Revelation 17:1-6)

The great whore of Babylon – who is she?

In chapter 13 we saw that the Beast's kingdom will be a restored form of the old Roman empire. Here in Revelation chapter 17 we are introduced to the *great whore that sitteth upon many waters*. Let us explore the clues to her identity:

- The *great whore that sitteth upon many [1]waters*, means that she has worldwide influence.

- She has such worldwide influence that *the kings of the earth have committed fornication* with her. The *great whore* is *that great city, which reigneth over the kings of the earth*, therefore physical fornication is not possible since you cannot commit physical fornication with a city. The meaning here is [2]spiritual fornication, which means that the *whore* practices idolatry.

- *the inhabitants of the earth have been made drunk with the wine of her fornication*, meaning that the people of the earth have been drawn in and intoxicated with her idolatrous practices. This suggests that the followers of the *great whore* are devout idolatrous worshippers.

- *I saw a woman sit upon a scarlet coloured beast, full of names of blasphemy, having [3]seven heads and ten horns.* The *woman* rides on the back of the Beast. The Beast's kingdom is a restored form of the old Roman empire, therefore taking into account the above points too, the *great whore* is a powerful religious element of Rome. The *great whore* is obviously the Roman Catholic Church. There is a double meaning here: the fact that the

---

[1]Revelation 17:15: *The waters which thou sawest, where the whore sitteth, are peoples, and multitudes, and nations, and tongues.*

[2]See chapter 2: *2) to commit fornication (Revelation 2:14)*

[3]The seven heads and ten horns aspect of the Beast were dealt with in chapter 13 and shows that the Beast's kingdom will be a restored form the old Roman empire.

woman rides on the back of the Beast also means that the Beast will support the woman, at least [4]initially.

- *The woman was arrayed in purple and scarlet colour, and decked with gold and precious stones and pearls.* The *woman* is expensively dressed and is obviously very rich.

- *the woman* [had] *a golden cup in her hand full of abominations and filthiness of her fornication.* The *golden cup* shows that outwardly she appears to be good; but the cup is *full of abominations and filthiness of her fornication* – inside the cup is corruption, indicating that despite an outward show of splendour, inwardly the *woman* is actually abominable and filthy.

- *And upon her forehead was a name written, MYSTERY, BABYLON THE GREAT, THE MOTHER OF HARLOTS AND ABOMINATIONS OF THE EARTH.* Babylon was where idolatry started. The Babylonian empire was conquered by the Medes and Persians. They were conquered by the Macedonians, who were in turn conquered by the Romans. Rome therefore succeeded to the power of Babylon and in the Roman empire, the idolatrous worship of the conquered nations continued. Therefore Rome is *that great city which reigneth over the kings of the earth (Revelation 17:18).*

---

[4]The events of Revelation chapter 18 are due to the Beast and the ten kingdoms of his empire attacking the Roman Catholic Church: *And the ten horns which thou sawest upon the beast, these shall hate the whore, and shall make her desolate and naked, and shall eat her flesh, and burn her with fire. For God hath put in their hearts to fulfil his will, and to agree, and give their kingdom unto the beast, until the words of God shall be fulfilled. (Revelation 17:16-17)*

- *And I saw the woman drunken with the blood of the saints, and with the blood of the martyrs of Jesus.* This is evidently a reference to Rome's persecution of true believers. From the cruel persecution of the early Christians who were thrown to the lions and used as human torches for Roman banquets, through to more modern times when the Roman Catholic Church persecuted Protestants and burnt many of them at the stake. The *woman* is indeed *drunken with the blood of the saints, and with the blood of the martyrs of Jesus.*

To recap, the great whore of Babylon:

- Has worldwide influence.

- Is religious and practices spiritual fornication.

- Has drawn people of all nations and caused them to practice idolatry also.

- Is based at Rome:

  And here is the mind which hath wisdom. The seven heads are [5]seven mountains, on which the woman sitteth (Revelation 17:9).

  the woman whom thou sawest is that great city which reigneth over the kings of the earth (Revelation 17:18).

- Rides the Beast, and is supported by him.

- Is very rich and gorgeously apparelled.

---

[5]Rome is built on seven hills.

- Outwardly looks good but inwardly is full of abomination and filthiness.

- Has persecuted true believers throughout its history.

Let us now see if 'the cap fits' the Roman Catholic Church. Some of the above points have not yet taken place, but we can concentrate on past events:

- The Roman Catholic Church is worldwide (Revelation 17:1, 15, 18).

- The Roman Catholic Church commits spiritual fornication – instead of recognising the Lord Jesus Christ as the head of the church, the Pope is held as the supreme head of the church. They [6]worship icons and Mary and pray to her, even though the Bible makes it clear that no-one except God is worthy of worship or prayer. The Pope also allows people to worship him.

---

[6]Worship is for God alone. It is sinful (idolatry) to worship any created being:

Exodus 34:14 *thou shalt worship no other god: for the LORD, whose name is Jealous, is a jealous God...*

Matthew 4:10 *Then saith Jesus unto him, Get thee hence, Satan: for it is written, Thou shalt worship the Lord thy God, and him only shalt thou serve.*

Worship was refused by Peter: *And as Peter was coming in, Cornelius met him, and fell down at his feet, and worshipped him. But Peter took him up, saying, Stand up; I myself also am a man. (Acts 10:25-26)*

Worship was refused by an angel: *And I John saw these things, and heard them. And when I had heard and seen, I fell down to worship before the feet of the angel which shewed me these things. Then saith he unto me, See thou do it not: for I am thy fellowservant, and of thy brethren the prophets, and of them which keep the sayings of this book: worship God. (Revelation 22:8-9).*

- The Roman Catholic Church is outwardly seen to do good but inwardly is corrupt.

- The Roman Catholic Church is very rich.

- The Roman Catholic Church is based at Rome.

18

Revelation chapter 18:
The whore's destruction

And after these things I saw another angel come down from heaven, having great power; and the earth was lightened with his glory. And he cried mightily with a strong voice, saying, Babylon the great is fallen, is fallen, and is become the habitation of devils, and the hold of every foul spirit, and a cage of every unclean and hateful bird. For all nations have drunk of the wine of the wrath of her fornication, and the kings of the earth have committed fornication with her, and the merchants of the earth are waxed rich through the abundance of her delicacies. (Revelation 18:1-3)

The angel who proclaims Babylon's (i.e. Rome's) downfall can only be the Lord Jesus Christ because the [1]*earth was lightened with his glory*. Babylon first falls spiritually, then physically. Verses 2 and 3 testify that Babylon has fallen spiritually: it *is become the habitation of devils, and the hold of every foul spirit, and a cage of every unclean and hateful bird*. In Revelation 13:11 we are introduced to the false prophet who causes men to worship the Beast and his image; refusal will mean death. Let me briefly recap on part of chapter 13:

---

[1]Jesus Christ is the light of the world (John 8:12)

And I beheld another beast coming up out of the earth; and he had two horns like a lamb, and he spake as a dragon. (Revelation 13:11)

The false prophet will come *out of the earth*, i.e. a well-established, stable environment. He has two horns, therefore he has two spheres of authority. He derives his political authority from the first (Antichrist) Beast (in Revelation 13:16, 17 he causes people *to receive a mark in their right hand, or in their foreheads... that no man might buy or sell, save he that had the mark* – political authority; and he causes the world to worship the Antichrist Beast – religious authority (Revelation 13:12)). Not only does he have two horns but he has *two horns <u>like a lamb</u>*. Jesus Christ is *the Lamb of God (John 1:29)*, and the false prophet <u>appears</u> to be Christ-like, but appearances are deceptive because the Bible says *he spake as a dragon*. He is Satanically inspired.

- The false prophet will come from a well-established, stable environment.

- He has two spheres of authority.

- He appears Christ-like, but is actually Satanically inspired.

Could this indicate that the false prophet will be a future Pope? Revelation chapters 17 and 18 refer to Rome, as do parts of other chapters. We have already seen how the Beast will be the leader of a restored Roman empire. We have seen that the Beast's seven heads refers to Rome: *...The seven heads are seven mountains... (Revelation 17:9)*. The false prophet has two spheres of authority: political and religious. The Pope has religious authority: the Roman Catholic Church, and he also has political authority: he governs Vatican City.

So far, I have speculated that the false prophet could be a future pope of the Roman Catholic Church. The false prophet is the Beast's religious leader and he is used by the Beast to set up a worldwide false 'church' which forces people to worship the Beast and the image of the Beast on penalty of death for refusal. Let me recap some more of Chapter 13:

And he [the false prophet] *exerciseth all the power of the first beast before him, and causeth the earth and them which dwell therein to worship the first beast, whose deadly wound was healed. And he doeth great wonders, so that he maketh fire come down from heaven on the earth in the sight of men, And deceiveth them that dwell on the earth by the means of those miracles which he had power to do in the sight of the beast; saying to them that dwell on the earth, that they should make an image to the beast, which had the wound by a sword, and did live. And he had power to give life unto the image of the beast, that the image of the beast should both speak, and cause that as many as would not worship the image of the beast should be killed. (Revelation 13:12-15)*

The false prophet will exercise Satanic power to cause the world to worship the Beast. He will do this by deceiving people through signs and wonders. For example, he will cause fire to come down from Heaven. The false prophet will cause an image of the Beast to be made... then people will have a choice between worship of the image of the Beast and death!

The Roman Catholic Church is well known today for its worship of idols (icons and statues), so it is feasible for the false prophet to come from a Roman Catholic background. A church which practices such things will degrade itself even further once the Holy Spirit is removed from the world. A church such as this would regress very quickly. Indeed we are told that *Babylon the great is fallen, is fallen, and is become the habitation of devils, and the hold of every foul spirit, and a cage of every unclean and hateful bird (Revelation 18:2)*; thus we see Babylon's spiritual fall.

And I heard another voice from heaven, saying, Come out of her, my people, that ye be not partakers of her sins, and that ye receive not of her plagues. (Revelation 18:4)

If the great whore of Babylon is the Roman Catholic Church then this verse tells us that it contains some true Christians; the Lord says *come out of her <u>my people</u>*. Christians are called out of the Roman Catholic Church so that they *be not partakers of her sins*. To worship according to Catholicism is to practise idolatry. Christians are called out so that they *receive not of her plagues. For her sins have reached unto heaven, and God hath remembered her iniquities (Revelation 18:4b-5)*.

Reward her even as she rewarded you, and double unto her double according to her works: in the cup which she hath filled fill to her double. How much she hath glorified herself, and lived deliciously, so much torment and sorrow give her: for she saith in her heart, I sit a queen, and am no widow, and shall see no sorrow. (Revelation 18:6-7)

Those who have been persecuted, tortured and killed in the name of the Roman Catholic Church are called to give a double amount back. The wording here is deliberately similar to Isaiah's prophecy of the judgement of literal Babylon which God administered through the [2]Medes and Persians: *thou saidst, I shall be a lady for ever... Therefore hear now this, thou that art given to pleasures, that dwellest carelessly, that sayest in*

---

[2]Recorded in Daniel chapter 5. It is God who *removeth kings, and setteth up kings (Daniel 2:21)*

thine heart, I am, and none else beside me; I shall not sit as a widow, neither shall I know the loss of children: But these two things shall come to thee in a moment in one day, the loss of children, and widowhood: they shall come upon thee in their perfection for the multitude of thy sorceries, and for the great abundance of thine enchantments. (Isaiah 47:7-9). Just as literal Babylon practised idolatry and thought itself invincible and everlasting, so too does Roman Catholicism, both in the sense of a continuation of power because Rome succeeded to the power of Babylon and also in its own right through its own history and traditions.

Therefore shall her plagues come in one day, death, and mourning, and famine; and she shall be utterly burned with fire: for strong is the Lord God who judgeth her. And the kings of the earth, who have committed fornication and lived deliciously with her, shall bewail her, and lament for her, when they shall see the smoke of her burning, Standing afar off for the fear of her torment, saying, Alas, alas, that great city Babylon, that mighty city! for in one hour is thy judgment come. (Revelation 18:8-10)

Rome's physical downfall will be sudden. Verse 8 says *her plagues shall come in one day*, and verse 10 *in one hour*. Which is right, one day or one hour? The answer is both! 'one day' is literal; 'one hour' is an unspecified period of approximately 3½ years. Consider the following:

Daniel 9:27, *And he* [the Beast of Revelation chapter 13] *shall confirm the covenant with many for one week: and in the midst of the week he shall cause the sacrifice and the oblation to cease, and for the overspreading of abominations he shall make it desolate, even until the consummation, and that determined shall be poured upon the desolate.*

As discussed in chapter 13, this verse indicates that the Beast will sign a covenant with Israel for 'one week' (which is actually a 'week of years' or seven years) allowing them to worship according to the Mosaic law, but in the middle of the 'week' he will go back on this promise. At the same time he will turn on the Roman Catholic Church and destroy it: *And the ten horns which thou sawest upon the beast, these shall hate the whore, and shall make her desolate and naked, and shall eat her flesh, and burn her with fire. (Revelation 17:16).* Soon after this the Beast and his armies will be conquered by Christ at Armageddon. The ten kings of the Beast's restored Roman empire will *receive power <u>one hour</u> with the beast (Revelation 17:12)* and Rome's judgement will come in one hour (Revelation 18:10) and since it is Christ who deprives the Beast's ten kings of their power, then this 'hour' must be a period of approximately 3½ years. Thus, God will use the Beast to destroy Rome in *one day (Revelation 18:8)* and in *one [3]hour (Revelation 18:10).*

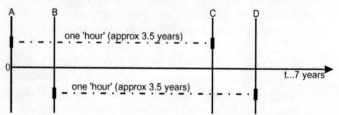

Figure 1 The tribulation period

---

[3] The 'hour' in Revelation 17:12 and Revelation 18:10 is an unspecified period of approximately 3½ years. The period of 'half an hour' mentioned in Revelation 8:1 is the Greek word 'hemiorion' which means literally 'half an hour'

A   The Beast makes a covenant with the Jews for seven years (Daniel 9:27).

B   The Beast becomes leader of the restored Roman empire (see chapter 13). Start of the ten kings reign *one hour with the beast (Revelation 17:10).*

C   The Beast breaks the covenant with the Jews after just 3½ years (Daniel 9:27).

He sits in the temple at Jerusalem and demands worship! (2 Thess 2:4; Mt 24:15 onward)

Also at this point he destroys Rome – Rome's 'hour' has finished.

D   The tribulation period 'week' is cut short by Christ's return at Armageddon (Revelation ch 19).

For then shall be great tribulation, such as was not since the beginning of the world to this time, no, nor ever shall be. And except those days should be shortened, there should no flesh be saved: but for the elect's sake those days shall be shortened. (Matthew 24:21-22).

The ten kings 'hour'-long reign with the Beast is finished.

The rest of this chapter really needs no explanation:

And the merchants of the earth shall weep and mourn over her; for no man buyeth their merchandise any more: The merchandise of gold, and silver, and precious stones, and of pearls, and fine linen, and purple, and silk, and scarlet, and all thyine wood, and all manner vessels of ivory, and all manner vessels of most precious wood, and of brass, and iron, and

*marble, And cinnamon, and odours, and ointments, and
frankincense, and wine, and oil, and fine flour, and wheat, and
beasts, and sheep, and horses, and chariots, and slaves, and
souls of men. And the fruits that thy soul lusted after are
departed from thee, and all things which were dainty and goodly
are departed from thee, and thou shalt find them no more at all.
The merchants of these things, which were made rich by her,
shall stand afar off for the fear of her torment, weeping and
wailing, And saying, Alas, alas, that great city, that was clothed
in fine linen, and purple, and scarlet, and decked with gold, and
precious stones, and pearls! For in one hour so great riches is
come to nought. And every shipmaster, and all the company in
ships, and sailors, and as many as trade by sea, stood afar off,
And cried when they saw the smoke of her burning, saying,
What city is like unto this great city! And they cast dust on their
heads, and cried, weeping and wailing, saying, Alas, alas, that
great city, wherein were made rich all that had ships in the sea
by reason of her costliness! for in one hour is she made
desolate. Rejoice over her, thou heaven, and ye holy apostles
and prophets; for God hath avenged you on her. And a mighty
angel took up a stone like a great millstone, and cast it into the
sea, saying, Thus with violence shall that great city Babylon be
thrown down, and shall be found no more at all. And the voice
of harpers, and musicians, and of pipers, and trumpeters, shall
be heard no more at all in thee; and no craftsman, of
whatsoever craft he be, shall be found any more in thee; and the
sound of a millstone shall be heard no more at all in thee; And
the light of a candle shall shine no more at all in thee; and the
voice of the bridegroom and of the bride shall be heard no more
at all in thee: for thy merchants were the great men of the
earth; for by thy sorceries were all nations deceived. And in her
was found the blood of prophets, and of saints, and of all that
were slain upon the earth. And after these things I heard a great
voice of much people in heaven, saying, Alleluia; Salvation, and
glory, and honour, and power, unto the Lord our God: For true
and righteous are his judgments: for he hath judged the great*

*whore, which did corrupt the earth with her fornication, and
hath avenged the blood of his servants at her hand. And again
they said, Alleluia. And her smoke rose up for ever and ever.
And the four and twenty elders and the four beasts fell down
and worshipped God that sat on the throne, saying, Amen;
Alleluia. (Revelation 18:11-19:4)*

19

Revelation chapter 19:
The marriage of the Lamb and Armageddon!

The marriage of the Lamb

And I heard as it were the voice of a great multitude, and as the
voice of many waters, and as the voice of mighty thunderings,
saying, Alleluia: for the Lord God omnipotent reigneth. Let us be
glad and rejoice, and give honour to him: for the marriage of the
Lamb is come, and his wife hath made herself ready.
(Revelation 19:6-7)

At the marriage of the Lamb, the bride of Christ is His church.
The marriage is a symbol of the completed spiritual unity
between Christ and His church. The church is ready, not on its
own merit, but because of what Christ has done by dying on the
cross at Calvary:

John 3:16 *For God so loved the world, that he gave his only*
begotten Son, that whosoever believeth in him should not
perish, but have everlasting life.

1 Thessalonians 4:14 *For if we believe that Jesus died and rose*
again, even so them also which sleep in Jesus will God bring
with him.

John 6:27 *Labour not for the meat which perisheth, but for that*
meat which endureth unto everlasting life, which the Son of man
shall give unto you: for him hath God the Father sealed.

John 6:29 *This is the work of God, that ye believe on him whom he hath sent.*

John 6:35 *Jesus said unto them, I am the bread of life: he that cometh to me shall never hunger; and he that believeth on me shall never thirst.*

The church is also ready because she has been tried by fire as described in 1 Corinthians chapter 3: *According to the grace of God which is given unto me, as a wise masterbuilder, I have laid the foundation, and another buildeth thereon. But let every man take heed how he buildeth thereupon. For other foundation can no man lay than that is laid, which is Jesus Christ. Now if any man build upon this foundation gold, silver, precious stones, wood, hay, stubble; Every man's work shall be made manifest: for the day shall declare it, because it shall be revealed by fire; and the fire shall try every man's work of what sort it is. If any man's work abide which he hath built thereupon, he shall receive a reward. If any man's work shall be burned, he shall suffer loss: but he himself shall be saved; yet so as by fire. (1 Corinthians 3:10-15)*

Because no sin or uncleanness can enter into God's presence, when the Lord comes for Christians at the rapture and we meet Him in the air, all sin remaining in our nature will be taken from us, leaving just the pure, Christ-like parts of our nature. The *man's work* referred to here is the spiritual work of developing our Christian character; the more we develop our Christian character (the more Christ-like we become) the greater will be our ability to do the Lord's work here on earth because our ability to perceive what the Lord would have us to do will be greater. At the rapture, Christians will be given a [1]glorious new

---

[1] 1 Corinthians ch 15

body which will be immortal and incorruptible. We will be given this new body because no sin or uncleanness can enter God's presence. When we are given our new bodies we will still recognise each other: *For now we see through a glass, darkly; but then face to face: now I know in part; but then shall I know even as also I am known (1 Corinthians 13:12)*. It is important to develop our Christian character for another reason: the refining process described in 1 Corinthians chapter 3 will burn up everything in our character that is ungodly. If we have not taken the trouble to develop our Christian character we may not have much of a character left when we have been refined! As 1 Corinthians 3:15 says: *If any mans work shall be burned, he shall suffer loss: but he himself shall be saved; yet so as by fire.*

And to her was granted that she should be arrayed in fine linen, clean and white: for the fine linen is the righteousness of saints. (Revelation 19:8)

The *fine linen, clean and white* is symbolic of casting off sin and putting on righteousness. This is illustrated in Zechariah 3:4, *And he answered and spake unto those that stood before him, saying, Take away the filthy garments from him. And unto him he said, Behold, I have caused thine iniquity to pass from thee, and I will clothe thee with change of raiment.*

And he saith unto me, Write, Blessed are they which are called unto the marriage supper of the Lamb. (Revelation 19:9)

The literal translation of the word *Blessed* is 'Happy', which describes those who are *called to the marriage supper of the Lamb*. These are not the bride but will be Old Testament saints and all New Testament saints who have died before the ascension of Christ (John the Baptist for example). The marriage supper of the Lamb is a celebration of the completed union between Christ and His church.

Armageddon

The name 'Armageddon' comes from Revelation 16:16 and is generally accepted to be the mountain of Megiddo to the north of the plain of Jezreel. This has been the scene for many battles recorded in the Bible. It may be significant that this is also the area just north of the much disputed West Bank and south of the equally disputed Golan Heights.

And I saw heaven opened, and behold a white horse; and he that sat upon him was called Faithful and True, and in righteousness he doth judge and make war. His eyes were as a flame of fire, and on his head were many crowns; (Revelation 19:11-12a)

The one sitting on a white horse is Christ. The white horse is symbolic of justice and holiness. We are told that Christ is *called Faithful and True, and in righteousness he doth judge and make war (Revelation 19:11)*. Christ's victory is assured because He is *Faithful and True* to the will of God: *Let this mind be in you, which was also in Christ Jesus: Who, being in the form of God, thought it not robbery to be equal with God: But made himself of no reputation, and took upon him the form of a servant, and was made in the likeness of men: And being found in fashion as a man, he humbled himself, and became obedient unto death, even the death of the cross. Wherefore God also hath highly exalted him, and given him a name which is above every name: That at the name of Jesus every knee should bow, of things in heaven, and things in earth, and things under the earth; And that every tongue should confess that Jesus Christ is Lord, to the glory of God the Father. (Philippians 2:5-11)*.

Christ is the judge of mankind. His righteous judgement is symbolised by *His eyes ...as a flame of fire (Revelation 19:12)*. When on Earth Christ said: *the Father judgeth no man, but hath*

committed all judgment unto the Son (John 5:22). The Apostle
Paul said: *he* [Christ] *commanded us to preach unto the people,
and to testify that it is he which was ordained of God to be the
Judge of quick* [the living] *and dead (Acts 10:42),* and: *he* [God]
*hath appointed a day, in the which he will judge the world in
righteousness by that man* [Christ] *whom he hath ordained;
whereof he hath given assurance unto all men, in that he hath
raised him from the dead (Acts 17:31).*

The crowns that the Lord wears on His head (Revelation 19:12)
are, the Greek 'diadema' which are the crowns of a king.

**and he had a name written, that no man knew, but he himself
(Revelation 19:12b)**

The Lord Jesus Christ has a name that is known only to
Himself. It is interesting that believers too will receive such a
name: ...*To him that overcometh will I give to eat of the hidden
manna, and will give him a white stone, and in the stone a new
name written, which no man knoweth saving he that receiveth it
(Revelation 2:17).*

**And he was clothed with a vesture dipped in blood: and his name
is called The Word of God. And the armies which were in heaven
followed him upon white horses, clothed in fine linen, white and
clean. (Revelation 19:13-14)**

Whether the blood that His outer garment is dipped in is
symbolic of His own blood by which he purchased mankind's
salvation, or whether it is symbolic of the blood of the Beast
and his armies against whom He now rides is unclear.

His name *the* [2]*Word of God* is descriptive of Christ's existence in the beginning with God, as God the Son. It shows His participation in the creation of the universe and His incarnation on earth, born to a virgin, Mary, as Christ the Saviour of mankind.

He is followed toward Armageddon by armies of saints. Jesus showed His second coming from the viewpoint of those in the world in Matthew 24:29-31: *Immediately after the tribulation of those days shall the sun be darkened, and the moon shall not give her light, and the stars shall fall from heaven, and the powers of the heavens shall be shaken: And then shall appear the sign of the Son of man in heaven: and then shall all the tribes of the earth mourn, and they shall see the Son of man coming in the clouds of heaven with power and great glory. And he shall send his angels with a great sound of a trumpet, and they shall gather together his elect from the four winds, from one end of heaven to the other.*

---

[2] See John 1:1-14

And out of his mouth goeth a sharp sword, that with it he should smite the nations: and he shall rule them with a rod of iron: and he treadeth the winepress of the fierceness and wrath of Almighty God. And he hath on his vesture and on his thigh a name written, KING OF KINGS, AND LORD OF LORDS. And I saw an angel standing in the sun; and he cried with a loud voice, saying to all the fowls that fly in the midst of heaven, Come and gather yourselves together unto the supper of the great God; That ye may eat the flesh of kings, and the flesh of captains, and the flesh of mighty men, and the flesh of horses, and of them that sit on them, and the flesh of all men, both free and bond, both small and great. (Revelation 19:15-18)

Christ's battle weapon is His word. Although the kings of the earth will no doubt have their weapons ready, this battle will be won by the word of Christ. The powerful word of Christ is capable of [3]creating the universe that we live in and is capable of overcoming the Beast and his armies. We may not understand the power by which these things can be done, but nevertheless we have the evidence of the created universe to show us that it is so.

Christ *treadeth the winepress of the fierceness and wrath of Almighty God (Revelation 19:15)*. The winepress is a symbol of divine judgement. [4]It is not wine that comes out of this winepress; it is the blood of the armies of the Beast.There is no doubt but that Christ will be victorious. This is clearly shown by the angel gathering the fowls to be ready to [5]devour the flesh of those about to be slain!

---

[3]John 1:3,10; Genesis chapter 1

[4]See the narrative on Revelation 14:12-20 for more details.

[5]Compare Ezekiel 39:17-20

The reference to Christ's rule: *he shall rule them with a rod of iron (Revelation 19:15)* is a reference to Christ's 1000 year reign on earth, which follows the battle of Armageddon. This was prophesied in Psalm 2:8-12: *Ask of me, and I shall give thee the heathen for thine inheritance, and the uttermost parts of the earth for thy possession. Thou shalt break them with a rod of iron; thou shalt dash them in pieces like a potter's vessel. Be wise now therefore, O ye kings: be instructed, ye judges of the earth. Serve the LORD with fear, and rejoice with trembling. Kiss the Son, lest he be angry, and ye perish from the way, when his wrath is kindled but a little. Blessed are all they that put their trust in him.*

And I saw the beast, and the kings of the earth, and their armies, gathered together to make war against him that sat on the horse, and against his army. And the beast was taken, and with him the false prophet that wrought miracles before him, with which he deceived them that had received the mark of the beast, and them that worshipped his image. These both were cast alive into a lake of fire burning with brimstone. And the remnant were slain with the sword of him that sat upon the horse, which sword proceeded out of his mouth: and all the fowls were filled with their flesh. (Revelation 19:19-21)[6]

The lake of fire is what is commonly referred to as Hell, the place reserved for Satan and his demons. The Beast and false prophet are captured at the battle of Armageddon. All unbelievers will be judged after Christ's 1000 year reign on earth, with this exception: the Beast and the false prophet are

---

[6]This fulfils Daniel 2:34. Daniel 2:35 is fulfilled by Christ's 1000 year reign

judged at the battle of Armageddon, are condemned to everlasting torment in the fires of Hell, and accordingly are *cast alive into a lake of fire burning with brimstone.*

20

Revelation chapter 20:
Christ's 1000 year rule;
judgement of the great white throne

And I saw an angel come down from heaven, having the key of the bottomless pit and a great chain in his hand. And he laid hold on the dragon, that old serpent, which is the Devil, and Satan, and bound him a thousand years, And cast him into the bottomless pit, and shut him up, and set a seal upon him, that he should deceive the nations no more, till the thousand years should be fulfilled: and after that he must be loosed a little season. (Revelation 20:1-3)

Following Christ's victory at the battle of Armageddon, Satan is bound for 1000 years in the [1]bottomless pit. Mankind will not be deceived by Satan during Christ's rule on earth. The angel who *laid hold on ...Satan, and bound him a thousand years, And cast him into the bottomless pit* must surely be the Lord Jesus Christ Himself. It is hard to believe that an ordinary angel has the power and authority to imprison Satan (in the book of Jude, the archangel Michael did not dare to even bring an accusation against Satan, much less to actually lay hands on him: *Yet Michael the archangel, when contending with the devil he disputed about the body of Moses, durst not bring against him a railing accusation, but said, The Lord rebuke thee. (Jude 1:9)*

---

[1]See notes in chapter 9.

Revelation chapter 20:
Christ's 1000 year rule;
judgement of the great white throne

And I saw thrones, and they sat upon them, and judgment was given unto them: and I saw the souls of them that were beheaded for the witness of Jesus, and for the word of God, and which had not worshipped the beast, neither his image, neither had received his mark upon their foreheads, or in their hands; and they lived and reigned with Christ a thousand years. But the rest of the dead lived not again until the thousand years were finished. This is the first resurrection. Blessed and holy is he that hath part in the first resurrection: on such the second death hath no power, but they shall be priests of God and of Christ, and shall reign with him a thousand years. (Revelation 20:4-6)

The thrones

The thrones are twenty-four in number: *And round about the throne were four and twenty seats: and upon the seats I saw four and twenty elders sitting, clothed in white raiment; and they had on their heads crowns of gold. (Revelation 4:4).*

Among those who sit upon the thrones are the twelve apostles: *And Jesus said unto them* [the apostles], *Verily I say unto you. That ye which have followed me, in the regeneration when the Son of man shall sit in the throne of his glory, ye also shall sit upon twelve thrones, judging the twelve tribes of Israel (Matthew 19:28).* The other twelve could be representatives of the twelve tribes of Israel. In Revelation chapter 21 we are told that New Jerusalem will have *twelve gates... and names written thereon, which are the names of the twelve tribes of the children of Israel (Revelation 21:12)*; *And the wall of the city had twelve foundations, and in them the names of the twelve apostles of the Lamb (Revelation 21:14).*

Revelation chapter 20:
Christ's 1000 year rule;
judgement of the great white throne

The two resurrections

There are basically two resurrections spoken of at this time in
the earth's history. They are summed up by John 5:28-29: *...the
hour is coming, in the which all that are in the graves shall hear
his voice, And shall come forth; they that have done good, unto
the resurrection of life; and they that have done evil, unto the
resurrection of damnation.*

The first resurrection

Those who have their part in the first resurrection and who *shall
be priests of God and of Christ, and shall reign with him a
thousand years (Revelation 20:6)*, are:

- The church and Old Testament believers, who will be
  translated at the rapture, before the tribulation period
  (1 Thess 4:16-17).

- Those who are killed for their new-found faith in the
  Lord Jesus Christ during the tribulation period. These are
  those who are *under the altar* in Revelation 6:9-11.
  These will be raised to life at the start of Christ's
  1000 year reign.

The second resurrection (the second death)

We are told in Revelation 20:5 that *the rest of the dead lived not
again until the thousand years were finished*. These are those
whose names are not written in the book of life. They must
endure the second death. Notice the exact wording: the second
death is not the oblivion that the ungodly hope for. The second

Revelation chapter 20:
Christ's 1000 year rule;
judgement of the great white throne

death is a raising to life: a [2]life of everlasting torment: *the rest of the dead lived not again until the thousand years were finished.*

And death and hell were cast into the lake of fire. This is the second death (Revelation 20:14)

And whosoever was not found written in the book of life was cast into the lake of fire. (Revelation 20:15)

Who will Christ reign over for 1000 years?

Initially these will consist of those who have come to believe in the Lord Jesus Christ during the tribulation period. There will of course be marriages and the birth of children so that the earth will soon be restocked with people. At the end of the 1000 year reign, those who remain alive will only be the righteous; all those who were deceived by Satan will be devoured by fire from Heaven (Revelation 20:9). [3]We are not told whether people will die from old age during Christ's earthly reign or whether people will once again attain the ages of those of the pre-flood earth. This is a detail that the Bible does not directly reveal to us.

---

[2]See notes in chapter 6 under the heading 'What Is It Like in Gehenna?'

[3]It must be the case that no one dies during this period because otherwise people would go through their whole life without being tempted by Satan: temptation is the prerequisite of choice: you cannot choose to follow God if you have no knowledge of an alternative: hence the reason why Adam and Eve had to be tempted (tested) by Satan.

Revelation chapter 20:
Christ's 1000 year rule;
judgement of the great white throne

What will life be like during Christ's 1000 year reign?

[4]Isaiah chapter 11 gives us a glimpse of life during this period. Christ's influence in the earth will extend even to the animal kingdom as can be seen from Isaiah 11:6-9, *The wolf also shall dwell with the lamb, and the leopard shall lie down with the kid; and the calf and the young lion and the fatling together; and a little child shall lead them. And the cow and the bear shall feed; their young ones shall lie down together: and the lion shall eat straw like the ox. And the sucking child shall play on the hole of the asp, and the weaned child shall put his hand on the cockatrice' den. They shall not hurt nor destroy in all my holy mountain: for the earth shall be full of the knowledge of the LORD, as the waters cover the sea.*

Zechariah also gives us a few details of life during Christ's 1000 year reign: *And the LORD shall be king over all the earth: in that day shall there be one LORD, and his name one. All the land shall be turned as a plain from Geba to Rimmon south of Jerusalem: and it shall be lifted up, and inhabited in her place, from Benjamin's gate unto the place of the first gate, unto the corner gate, and from the tower of Hananeel unto the king's winepresses. And men shall dwell in it, and there shall be no more utter destruction; but Jerusalem shall be safely inhabited. (Zechariah 14:9-11)*

---

[4]Isaiah chapter 11 takes us through from Christ's first advent (verses 1-3); Christ's victory at the battle of Armageddon (verse 4); Christ's 1000 year reign on earth (Isaiah 11:5 - 12:6).

Revelation chapter 20:
Christ's 1000 year rule;
judgement of the great white throne

And when the thousand years are expired, Satan shall be loosed out of his prison, And shall go out to deceive the nations which are in the four quarters of the earth, Gog and Magog, to gather them together to battle: the number of whom is as the sand of the sea. And they went up on the breadth of the earth, and compassed the camp of the saints about, and the beloved city: and fire came down from God out of heaven, and devoured them. And the devil that deceived them was cast into the lake of fire and brimstone, where the beast and the false prophet are, and shall be tormented day and night for ever and ever. (Revelation 20:7-10)

There will be those who are dissatisfied with Christ's rule. The nature of ordinary mankind will still be sinful, even during Christ's reign on earth. There will be no uprising however, because there will be none who dare to oppose His rule. None that is, until Satan, the tempter of mankind, is loosed from the bottomless pit at the end of 1000 years of Christ's rule. All mankind would follow Christ during His actual, physical reign on earth because they really have no option. To legitimately make a choice to follow Christ, mankind needs to be tempted; unless mankind is given an alternative, the <u>choice</u> to follow Christ is meaningless. Accordingly, Satan is released to give mankind that choice.

Satan will deceive vast numbers of people and gather them to Jerusalem where they will surround the city. *Gog and Magog* seem to be the prince and people of a northern race, possibly the Scythians. God will deal swiftly with these turncoats and will strike them down with fire from Heaven. Satan will then be *cast into the lake of fire and brimstone, where the beast and the false prophet are, and shall be tormented day and night for ever and ever.*

Zechariah gives us more details of God's judgement on those who will be deceived by Satan:

Revelation chapter 20:
Christ's 1000 year rule;
judgement of the great white throne

And this shall be the plague wherewith the LORD will smite all the people that have fought against Jerusalem; Their flesh shall consume away while they stand upon their feet, and their eyes shall consume away in their holes, and their tongue shall consume away in their mouth. And it shall come to pass in that day, that a great tumult from the LORD shall be among them; and they shall lay hold every one on the hand of his neighbour, and his hand shall rise up against the hand of his neighbour. And Judah also shall fight at Jerusalem; and the wealth of all the heathen round about shall be gathered together, gold, and silver, and apparel, in great abundance. And so shall be the plague of the horse, of the mule, of the camel, and of the ass, and of all the beasts that shall be in these tents, as this plague. (Zechariah 14:12-15)

At first glance this does not seem to tie in with what we are told in Revelation, but consider what would happen when fire comes down from God and devours them. Burning flesh, eyes and tongue would certainly *consume away while they stand upon their feet.* Such an occurrence on this scale would induce mass terror to those afflicted which might explain Zechariah's statement that *a great tumult from the LORD shall be among them; and they shall lay hold every one on the hand of his neighbour, and his hand shall rise up against the hand of his neighbour.*

Revelation chapter 20:
Christ's 1000 year rule;
judgement of the great white throne

And I saw a great white throne, and him that sat on it, from whose face the earth and the heaven fled away; and there was found no place for them. And I saw the dead, small and great, stand before God; and the books were opened: and another book was opened, which is the book of life: and the dead were judged out of those things which were written in the books, according to their works. And the sea gave up the dead which were in it; and death and hell delivered up the dead which were in them: and they were judged every man according to their works. And death and hell were cast into the lake of fire. This is the second death. And whosoever was not found written in the book of life was cast into the lake of fire. (Revelation 20:11-15)

The *great white throne* is the final judgement of God. Its greatness is symbolic of its finality: there is no appeal against this judgement of God. Unlike in former times when God's judgement could be [5]turned by the prayer of the righteous, this judgement is final! The throne's whiteness symbolises the purity of God and His judgements.

...the earth and the heaven fled away; and there was found no place for them. This is the point at which this present Heaven and earth are destroyed. They have served their purpose and are needed no longer; Peter describes it like this: *But the day of the Lord will come as a thief in the night; in the which the heavens shall pass away with a great noise, and the elements shall melt with fervent heat, the earth also and the works that are therein shall be burned up... the heavens being on fire shall be dissolved, and the elements shall melt with fervent heat (2 Peter 3:10, 12).*

---

[5]An example of this is Exodus 32:7-14

Revelation chapter 20:
Christ's 1000 year rule;
judgement of the great white throne

The dead who are judged are those whose names are not written in the book of life. The other books contain a complete record of their lives. They have not accepted Christ as their Lord and Saviour and so they have not received forgiveness for their sins. They have to accept the penalty for their sins, whether small or great. The [6]punishment will fit the crime; they are *judged every man according to their works (Revelation 20:13)*.

And death and hell were cast into the lake of fire. This is the second death. And whosoever was not found written in the book of life was cast into the lake of fire (Revelation 20:14-15). All these unbelievers are assigned their permanent place of abode: the [7]lake of fire; the place of everlasting torment.

---

[6]See Luke 12:47-48

[7]See notes in chapter 6

21

Revelation chapter 21:
'Behold, I make all things new'

And I saw a new heaven and a new earth: for the first heaven and the first earth were passed away; and there was no more sea. And I John saw the holy city, new Jerusalem, coming down from God out of heaven, prepared as a bride adorned for her husband. (Revelation 21:1-2)

The old heaven and earth having been destroyed (Revelation 20:11), John sees a new heaven and a new earth.

...and there was no more sea: this curious declaration was given at a time when there were no charts of the seas or compasses to aid navigation. Sea travel was greatly feared and undertaken only when absolutely necessary. John's statement: *and there was no more sea* would have been a great comfort to his contemporaries. The real meaning however, is probably akin to that in Revelation chapter 13 where we see the Beast rise up out of the sea: the sea symbolising the tempestuous world political scene. In New Jerusalem the rule will not be that of sinful man but of a pure and holy God; and He will not rule over sinful men but over pure sinless translated saints.

And I John saw the holy city, new Jerusalem, coming down from God out of heaven, prepared as a bride adorned for her husband: this first sighting of the city, New Jerusalem, describes its beauty as being like a radiant bride on her wedding day.

And I heard a great voice out of heaven saying, Behold, the tabernacle of God is with men, and he will dwell with them, and they shall be his people, and God himself shall be with them, and be their God. And God shall wipe away all tears from their eyes; and there shall be no more death, neither sorrow, nor crying, neither shall there be any more pain: for the former things are passed away. (Revelation 21:3-4)

In Old Testament times the tabernacle was a visible reminder of God's presence. However, ordinary men were not allowed direct access to God in the 'most holy place' or 'holy of holies' behind the second veil. Here, the high priest only, was allowed once a year on the day of atonement. This was a picture of Christ's work of redemption on the cross. At Christ's death, the veil of the temple (a later, more permanent form of the tabernacle) was torn in two: *Jesus... yielded up the ghost. And, behold, the veil of the temple was rent in twain from the top to the bottom (Matthew 27:50-51)*. This signified that all believers now have direct access to God, in prayer, through the mediation of the Lord Jesus Christ. As the writer to the Hebrews has put it: we have *boldness to enter into the holiest by the blood of Jesus, By a new and living way, which he hath consecrated for us, through the veil, that is to say, his flesh (Hebrews 10:19-20)*. We cannot get any closer to God than this at present because we are still made of sinful flesh, and God being absolutely pure and holy, cannot have us in His presence; neither could we see the fulness of Him and live; it would be too much for us to bear. However, when we are taken up to be with the Lord, at the rapture of the church, our sinful nature will be taken away from us and our mortal, sinful bodies will be changed into immortal, incorruptible ones, and we shall at last be free of sin and able to stand in God's presence. No longer will our access to God be at a distance through our Mediator, the Lord Jesus Christ. God is actually going to dwell with us!

In the new order of things, *God shall wipe away all tears from their eyes; and there shall be no more death, neither sorrow, nor crying, neither shall there be any more pain: for the former things are passed away.* Sorrow, death, pain and suffering will be banished for ever.

And he that sat upon the throne said, Behold, I make all things new. And he said unto me, Write: for these words are true and faithful. And he said unto me, It is done. I am Alpha and Omega, the beginning and the end. I will give unto him that is athirst of the fountain of the water of life freely. He that overcometh shall inherit all things; and I will be his God, and he shall be my son. But the fearful, and unbelieving, and the abominable, and murderers, and whoremongers, and sorcerers, and idolaters, and all liars, shall have their part in the lake which burneth with fire and brimstone: which is the second death. (Revelation 21:5-8)

In the midst of this chapter of the future, God holds out the promise of eternal life: *I will give unto him that is athirst of the fountain of the water of life freely (Revelation 21:6)* to those who will *believe on him whom he hath sent (John 6:29).* There is no middle ground though; you cannot sit on the fence. If you believe, you will have your part in the new heaven and new earth. Those who will not make this commitment will be assigned *their part in the lake which burneth with fire and brimstone: which is the second death. (Revelation 21:8)*

*And there came unto me one of the seven angels which had the
seven vials full of the seven last plagues, and talked with me,
saying, Come hither, I will shew thee the bride, the Lamb's wife.
And he carried me away in the spirit to a great and high
mountain, and shewed me that great city, the holy Jerusalem,
descending out of heaven from God, Having the glory of God
(Revelation 21:9-11a)*

One of the angels *which had the seven vials full of the seven
last plagues* carries John to a great and high mountain to show
him *the bride, the Lamb's wife*. The angel shows John New
Jerusalem *descending out of heaven from God, Having the
glory of God* showing that everything that the saints [1] have, is
God given.

In the change of the Lamb's bride from the church to the city
of New Jerusalem, we are seeing what we commonly refer to
as Heaven. New Jerusalem symbolises the raptured church in
Heaven, where Saints will actually dwell with God in all His
fulness. When we are free from the shackles of sin we will be
able to not only endure the full glory of God, but to enjoy His
company, as Adam and Eve did in the beginning in the
Garden of Eden, before their disobedience which brought sin
into the world.

---

[1] Indeed, everything that the world has, is God given. The natural man will not, of
course, agree with this statement.

and her light was like unto a stone most precious, even like a jasper stone, clear as crystal; And had a wall great and high, and had twelve gates, and at the gates twelve angels, and names written thereon, which are the names of the twelve tribes of the children of Israel: On the east three gates; on the north three gates; on the south three gates; and on the west three gates. And the wall of the city had twelve foundations, and in them the names of the twelve apostles of the Lamb. (Revelation 21:11b-14)

The light in New Jerusalem is like the light that radiates from a precious stone. However the jasper stone described here does not resemble the jasper that we know today. The description is more like that of a diamond.

The wall is for security: Heaven is a safe place. The gates ensure [2]free access to all who have the right of entrance. Since there is no night (Revelation 21:25), there is no need of shutting the gates; they are however, guarded by angels, highlighting the security and sanctity of Heaven. The foundations of New Jerusalem are the twelve Apostles; the names of the twelve tribes of Israel are written on the gates; these both showing the heritage and foundation of the church.

---

[2]You will notice that there are twelve gates—three on each side—it doesn't matter which direction you come from. You could be from any country and from any background and still gain entrance to the city; just as long as you come through the pearl of great price which is the Lord Jesus Christ (see narrative on Revelation 21:15-23); there is no other way in. To enter the city you must have the New Life that comes from accepting Jesus Christ as your Lord and Saviour.

And he that talked with me had a golden reed to measure the city, and the gates thereof, and the wall thereof. And the city lieth foursquare, and the length is as large as the breadth: and he measured the city with the reed, twelve thousand furlongs. The length and the breadth and the height of it are equal. And he measured the wall thereof, an hundred and forty and four cubits, according to the measure of a man, that is, of the angel. And the building of the wall of it was of jasper: and the city was pure gold, like unto clear glass. And the foundations of the wall of the city were garnished with all manner of precious stones. The first foundation was jasper; the second, sapphire; the third, a chalcedony; the fourth, an emerald; The fifth, sardonyx; the sixth, sardius; the seventh, chrysolite; the eighth, beryl; the ninth, a topaz; the tenth, a chrysoprasus; the eleventh, a jacinth; the twelfth, an amethyst. And the twelve gates were twelve pearls; every several gate was of one pearl: and the street of the city was pure gold, as it were transparent glass. And I saw no temple therein: for the Lord God Almighty and the Lamb are the temple of it. And the city had no need of the sun, neither of the moon, to shine in it: for the glory of God did lighten it, and the Lamb is the light thereof. (Revelation 21:15-23)

The city is square and covers an area of 2,250,000 square miles, that is, 1500 miles along each of its four sides. The city is also 1500 miles high. We are not told what form it will take, but it might resemble a huge skyscraper. It is essentially a cube of 1500 miles along its length, width and height. The wall around the city is 144 cubits high (about 216 feet).

We should not perhaps take the dimensions and form of the city too literally. The description of it surely means that New Jerusalem is big enough for all the Saints, while the grandeur of its materials and design show the standard of care that God has for His saints. When He was on earth, the Lord Jesus Christ said: *In my Father's house are many mansions: if it were not so, I would have told you. I go to prepare a place for you. And if I go and prepare a place for you, I will come again, and receive you to myself; that where I am, there ye may be also (John 14:2-3).*

Entrance into the city is via the twelve gates in the wall. The gates are guarded by twelve angels; you will not be allowed in unless you have the right passport! Each gate is a single pearl. The Lord Jesus Christ said: *...the kingdom of heaven is like unto a merchant man, seeking goodly pearls: Who, when he had found one pearl of great price, went and sold all that he had, and bought it (Matthew 13:45-46).* The Lord Jesus Christ is that *pearl of great price.* The Lord Jesus Christ is the ONLY way into the city, showing that THERE IS ONLY ONE WAY TO HEAVEN; you cannot get in except by a gate made of a single pearl. You cannot get in unless you have the passport of New Life in Christ.

We can see here the way the Lord Jesus Christ will see His raptured church. He will see us as pure gold, just as the city is pure gold. The wall of the city is garnished with precious stones, showing that the Lord will look upon each one of us as a unique and precious gemstone; each lovely to behold, yet each one different and all radiating the light which comes from the Lamb. The light of the city does not come from sun or moon but *the glory of God did lighten it, and the Lamb is the light thereof (Revelation 21:23).*

And the nations of them which are saved shall walk in the light of it: and the kings of the earth do bring their glory and honour into it. And the gates of it shall not be shut at all by day: for there shall be no night there. And they shall bring the glory and honour of the nations into it. And there shall in no wise enter into it any thing that defileth, neither whatsoever worketh abomination, or maketh a lie: but they which are written in the Lamb's book of life. (Revelation 21:24-27)

All who are saved: both Old Testament and New Testament saints, will have their part in this city and will live in accordance with the will of God. There will be no inner struggle in this, as there is now with the [3]struggle of our own will against the will of the Holy Spirit who indwells Christians. Once again we are assured of the sanctity of Heaven: *there shall in no wise enter into it any thing that defileth, neither whatsoever worketh abomination, or maketh a lie: but they which are written in the Lamb's book of life (Revelation 21:27).*

---

[3]The Apostle Paul was no stranger to this. See Romans 7:22 onward.

22

Revelation chapter 22:
The river and tree of life

And he shewed me a pure river of water of life, clear as crystal, proceeding out of the throne of God and of the Lamb. In the midst of the street of it, and on either side of the river, was there the tree of life, which bare twelve manner of fruits, and yielded her fruit every month: and the leaves of the tree were for the healing of the nations. (Revelation 22:1-2)

The *pure river of water of life* comes from God the Father through the Lord Jesus Christ. Christ said in John 10:9, *I am the door: by me if any man enter in, he shall be saved.* The [1]*tree of life* is watered by the *river of water of life* and bares twelve

---

[1]**The tree of life.** When Adam and Eve were cast out of the Garden of Eden the tree of life was guarded to prevent their access to it (Genesis 3:23-24): it therefore must have been an essential part of their original immortality. The original tree of life would have been washed away by the flood of Noah's time (Genesis chapters 6-8). In New Jerusalem, the tree of life will once more be available and, again, must be an essential part of immortality. It is watered by the river of water of life. Whether or not the tree of life is a literal tree, it is surely also symbolic of the Lord Jesus Christ, who has described Himself in these terms:

I am the vine, ye are the branches: He that abideth in me, and I in him, the same bringeth forth much fruit: for without me ye can do nothing. (John 15:5)

whosoever drinketh of the water that I shall give him shall never thirst; but the water that I shall give him shall be in him a well of water springing up into everlasting life. (John 4:14)

kinds of fruit. There are twelve tribes and twelve Apostles. This could indicate that although sinless we will all retain our individuality and diversity of taste; Heaven caters for this, shown by the diversity of fruits borne by the tree of life. The leaves of the tree are for *the healing of the nations*. This does not mean that there is sickness in Heaven that needs healing. It is probably to indicate that although on earth the different nations warred and quarrelled with each other, in Heaven things will be different. The nations will live in Heaven in harmony. Cultural diversities will not separate as on earth, rather, these differences will be readily accepted, symbolised by the *leaves of the tree ... for the healing of the nations*.

And there shall be no more curse: but the throne of God and of the Lamb shall be in it; and his servants shall serve him: And they shall see his face; and his name shall be in their foreheads. (Revelation 22:3-4)

[2]Sin, the curse of mankind, will not exist in Heaven. Indeed sin cannot enter that realm. Saints will be able to serve their Lord perfectly, without the taint of sin on all that they do. Being sinless, they will be able to look upon God's face. They will have His name written in their foreheads, signifying that they belong to Him. This is in stark contrast to those who will go through the tribulation period and *receive a mark in their right hand, or in their foreheads: And that no man might buy or sell, save he that had the mark...of the beast (Revelation 13:16-17)*.

---

[2]See Revelation 21:27

And he said unto me, These sayings are faithful and true: and the Lord God of the holy prophets sent his angel to shew unto his servants the things which must shortly be done. Behold, I come quickly: blessed is he that keepeth the sayings of the prophecy of this book. And he saith unto me, Seal not the sayings of the prophecy of this book: for the time is at hand. And, behold, I come quickly; and my reward is with me, to give every man according as his work shall be. (Revelation 22:6-7,10,12)

These things were revealed to John and to us so that we are aware of *the things which must shortly be done*. We are encouraged and fortified by the Lord's words *Behold, I come quickly* and we are blessed if we take heed of this prophetic book. We will be rewarded according to our works. Belief alone is sufficient to secure our salvation; rewards are given for our works.

Although the book of Revelation is not sealed, more of its meaning becomes known to us as we start to see these things happening around us. God will further reveal these things to His people as the time for their fulfilment draws ever closer.

He that is unjust, let him be unjust still: and he which is filthy, let him be filthy still: and he that is righteous, let him be righteous still: and he that is holy, let him be holy still. (Revelation 22:11)

As the time for the fulfilment of these words approaches, the values and behaviour of men will become more deeply entrenched. The ungodly will become more ungodly and the godly will become more godly. This will be particularly noticeable in the ungodly when the Holy Spirit is removed from the world along with the church at the rapture.

I am Alpha and Omega, the beginning and the end, the first and the last. Blessed are they that do his commandments, that they may have right to the tree of life, and may enter in through the gates into the city. For without are dogs, and sorcerers, and whoremongers, and murderers, and idolaters, and whosoever loveth and maketh a lie. (Revelation 22:13-15)

God reminds us of who He is: He is the beginning and the ending of all things. As the Psalmist has said: *Thy throne is established of old: thou art from everlasting (Psalm 93:2)*. Once more we see the contrast between the godly and ungodly. The godly *have right to the tree of life, and may enter in through the gates into the city*, while the ungodly are outside the city; indeed they *have their part in the lake which burneth with fire and brimstone: which is the second death (Revelation 21:8)*.

I Jesus have sent mine angel to testify unto you these things in the churches. I am the root and the offspring of David, and the bright and morning star. And the Spirit and the bride say, Come. And let him that heareth say, Come. And let him that is athirst come. And whosoever will, let him take the water of life freely. (Revelation 22:16-17)

These things were sent *...unto the seven churches which are in Asia... (Revelation 1:11)* and now they are revealed to the present day church as part of the Bible. God is *...not willing that any should perish, but that all should come to repentance (2 Peter 3:9)*; so once again He extends His hand to whosoever will come: the Holy Spirit says *come*; the church says *come*; anyone who hears the word is encouraged to say *come*. The invitation can come from any quarter; the important thing is that people come – and believe in the Lord Jesus Christ for the salvation of their souls: *and let him that is athirst come. And whosoever will, let him take the water of life freely (Revelation 22:17)*.

For I testify unto every man that heareth the words of the prophecy of this book, If any man shall add unto these things, God shall add unto him the plagues that are written in this book: And if any man shall take away from the words of the book of this prophecy, God shall take away his part out of the book of life, and out of the holy city, and from the things which are written in this book. (Revelation 22:18-19)

There is a serious warning here not to add to, or take away from, any part of the book of Revelation. To do so has very serious consequences.

He which testifieth these things saith, Surely I come quickly. Amen. Even so, come, Lord Jesus. The grace of our Lord Jesus Christ be with you all. Amen. (Revelation 22:20-21)

Bibliography

Most of the material used in this book is taken from the notes of my original studies in Revelation for which I deliberately used no reference books, though I did discuss various Scriptures with Christian friends. Since then I have been influenced by books I have read and I have used certain reference books for their historical and geographical data. I hope the following is a complete list of books used, either directly or which have influenced my thinking, but I apologize if I have left off any book that I should have included.

Graham, Billy. *Approaching Hoofbeats*. London: Hodder and Stoughton, 1985.

Smith, William. *Smith's Bible Dictionary*. New Jersey: Jove Publications, 1980

Unger, Merrill F. *Unger's Bible Handbook*. Chicago: Moody Press, 1967.

Watson, Sidney. *The Mark of the Beast*. Edinburgh: B. McCall Barbour, 1989.

Wight, Fred H. *Manners and Customs of Bible Lands*. Chicago: Moody Press, 1983.

Young, Robert. *Analytical Concordance to the Holy Bible*. Guildford and London: Lutterworth Press, 1979.

Printed in the United Kingdom
by Lightning Source UK Ltd.
100074UKS00001B/82-99